Geezer

And the

Kid

Adventures in Flight

Ron Irwin

i

ISBN 978-0-6151-5811-2

This book is dedicated to

Kari Feline Irwin, daughter extraordinaire and without question my

absolute favorite co-pilot and travel companion

-   and –

Nenita Perez Irwin, the kind of woman every man dreams of and because of

inexplicable good fortune I have had as my wife for a quarter of a century

-   and –

Kimberly Kaula Irwin, Kari's big sister and a woman who has flown an airplane

entirely by herself and who constantly seeks adventure.

Table of Contents

The Idea... 1

Day One WHP – DAG... 7

Day Two DAG – IGM... 30

Day Three IGM – GCN... 56

Day Four GCN – 0V7... 77

Day Five 0V7 – DRO...114

Day Six DRO – GUP...159

Day Seven GUP – SEZ..187

Day Eight Sedona, Arizona..211

Day Nine SEZ – IFP...230

Day Ten IFP – WHP...251

Post Action Debrief..270

The Idea

I had just celebrated my sixty second birthday and frankly I wasn't all that happy. My father had passed away at age seventy two. If I matched him I had but ten short years left. My paternal grand father passed on in his late sixties and as I recalled so had my maternal grand father. None of this was all that much fun to consider. Plus I had just signed up for Social Security. Add it all up and I was confronted with one inescapable fact. I had reached official geezerdom. Now I don't feel, like a geezer. I have plenty of energy, I typically sleep well and I get lots of exercise. I still have most of my teeth and I tend to stand straight up. So I don't think I have the total geezer look just yet. But by gum start drawing social security and you are indeed a geezer. Plus for sometime now I have been routinely given "senior" discounts at most of the chain restaurants. Of course all this really means is that maybe for the very first time concepts such as mortality become glaringly evident. Yuck! Who wants that? Anyhow that's me, Geezer.

Now meet the Kid, my wonderful eleven year old bright eyed girl, Kari Irwin. Kari was just finishing up her fifth year of school and next year would be her first year of middle school. Now as most parents know it is somewhere in middle school that many a really wonderful child becomes possessed. Kari's sister Kimberly, for example, dove right off the deep end right around sixth grade. In fact it was on Kimberly's twelfth birthday that her halo fell off and horns instantly sprouted. To her true credit Kimberly has come a long way back into the world since then, but there is still a ways to go and there was that long stretch of misery.

So I wanted to do something really special with my daughter before she either lost her halo or I kicked the bucket. But what to do? Soon she would be involved in her favorite summer activity,

Showcamp. She loves to sing and dance and act and she gets to do

it all each summer. But there was about a two and a half week

break between the end of her regular school and the start of

Showcamp. That was my window of opportunity.

Coincidently a friend and instrument flight ground student of mine,

Darren Baird was going to Kingman, Arizona with intentions of

finishing his instrument rating at the Sheble Flight School. At first

I had planned on flying him there and then taking a trip with Kari,

stopping back ten days later to pick him up. That, however, did

not work out and Darren had to drive from Los Angeles to

Kingman.   Still the idea of a ten or so day trip with my daughter

had gained strong interest with both of us. Well truth be told at

first she didn't want to go. You see Kari is fine in an airplane and

in fact she actually likes to fly except when her mom and my

terrific wife Nenita starts in on her extreme irrational anti flying chatter. Then and only then does Kari balk at flying. But we were able to work around that problem by promising flight of not much more than one hour each day.

So off I went to plan the details of this event. I wanted every day to begin with a fairly short flight, never very much more than one hour which kept the distance down to around about one hundred nautical miles each day. Also, with the exception of a stop in Kingman, Arizona to check on how my friend was progressing with his instrument rating course, each destination was chosen with fun as well as a learning opportunities in mind. Even Kingman, Arizona did have some sights to see and things to learn. And I wanted to introduce Kari to both America's great southwest and also to the Native Americans, better known as American Indians who inhabit much of this geography. So with those criteria I laid out the plan.

On day one we flew to the Barstow – Daggett area where I would take her to Peggy Sue's Diner, a place I knew she would love because of her love of the performing arts. I would also take her to the Calico Ghost Town for a look back on American history. On day two we would take care of business in Kingman, Arizona. Day three was to be really special because we would both be looking at the Grand Canyon for the very first time and we would be doing it together. Day four was totally off the wall. In order to keep to my one hour a day rule I needed some place to stop between the Grand Canyon, Arizona and Durango, Colorado. A review of the aeronautical charts produced the town of Kayenta, Arizona. I quickly learned that Kayenta was actually right in the Navajo reservation. I also found out that it was near Monument Valley, but I honestly had no idea just how beautiful, profound and important Monument Valley was until we got there. Now that is the essence of exploration and adventure. Durango, Colorado

came the next day, day five and it too became much bigger than I
at first contemplated. Day six was Gallup, New Mexico a town of
minimal tourist interest but nevertheless a place of historic value
and a place for us to rest as we turned back towards our home.
Day seven took us to the sensational Sedona, Arizona a place I had
heard so much about but had never before been to. Kari and I
would discover Sedona together and we would spend two days
there. Day nine required a little bit longer trip to Bullhead City,
Arizona and Laughlin, Nevada. I had been there before but Kari
had not. After all those days in the heat and dust we both would
enjoy the dependable coolness of the many hotel casinos in
Laughlin. Finally on day ten we would take our longest trip yet,
about two hours from Laughlin back to our home airport the
Whiteman Airport in Los Angeles, CA.

My goal was to treat Kari to many very special experiences in a
very different way, mainly by private airplane travel with her dad.

At first I gained her somewhat tepid agreement but as we discussed it more and more she became very enthusiastic for which I became a very happy man. So plan made, aircraft ready and bags packed on the 21st day of June 2007 the Geezer and the Kid launched a short but exciting adventure. It is now our very great pleasure to share that adventure with the world. We sincerely hope that you enjoy it thoroughly as you join the Geezer and the Kid on a spectacular ten day adventure in flight.

Day One

WHP – DAG

(Whiteman Airport, Los Angeles, CA –to- Barstow Daggett Airport, CA)

99 NM 1.0 Hours

I t was the first day of summer and what better place to go than the middle of the Mojave Desert. Our bags were packed, the flight itineraries were in hand, I had cash and plastic in my pocket and enthusiasm was high. We were on our way. My lovely daughter Kari and I were setting off on a special father/daughter adventure of a lifetime. In just 10 short days we would visit six states of the American southwest, view over a quarter of a million miles of varied and stunning sights, meet many interesting people, fly more than 1200 nautical miles and drive more than 350 miles all while enjoying each others company. Anticipation was reaching peak.

While driving from our home to the Whiteman Airport I called and got an abbreviated briefing from Flight Service. The weather was warm and the briefer cautioned me about winds and turbulence over the desert but we were leaving early so that would not likely be a problem. However, he also cautioned me about Unmanned Vehicles flying in the vicinity of Victorville. That is becoming more and more of a problem over the Mojave. The only solution is to stay connected with either Joshua Approach Control or Los Angeles Center and keep a constant look out.

The preflight inspection was uneventful. We loaded and secured our modest luggage and then I plugged my chosen route into my GPS. The engine of our Cessna Cardinal N13HK started up flawlessly and we taxied out to the run up area for runway 12 at the Whiteman Airport. As we did the normal run up drill, checking the magnetos, propeller governor and so forth the Whiteman tower officially opened; it was 0800 local and Tony was in charge.

"Whiteman tower Cardinal one three hotel kilo ready at one two, left down wind departure" I said. "Cardinal one three hotel kilo cleared for take off runway one two" spoke Tony from the tower. I taxied the airplane onto the center line while double checking the gauges and the directional gyro. Everything looked exactly right so the power was applied and she began her take off roll until crossing 60 mph indicated airspeed and with a gentle pull on the yoke and she lifted serenely off of the runway. We had committed lift and it was grand. There was little feeling actually except for the usual total exhilaration. More than 42 years of committing lift and not once has it ever been boring. Today was, however, truly special because I was joined on the flight with my favorite copilot, my 11 year old daughter Kari.

At 1400 feet indicated on our altimeter we banked gently left until we were heading 030 degrees. Continuing to climb we soon turned downwind from Whiteman to an initial heading of 300 degrees. At 2500 feet above sea level we were approaching the San Fernando Reservoir, I asked for and received permission from Whiteman tower to change our frequency from the Whiteman Tower frequency of 135.00 to the SoCal TRACON frequency of 120.40

and then I called SoCal. SoCal gave us a discreet squawk code and confirmed radar contact and we were solidly on our way.

All those familiar sights; the Hansen Dam and Hansen Dam Golf Course, the UPS facility and the 210 freeway to our right, San Fernando Road, the San Fernando Mission and the San Fernando Reservoir to our left, and the Newhall Pass basically straight ahead. The sun was bright; the sky was blue and the ride smooth as silk, a perfect start to a great excursion. Soon there were more familiar sights

As we crossed Newhall Pass we saw Magic Mountain Amusement park ahead and slightly left. Banking right we soon saw a flashing blue light on our instrument panel and heard a rhythmic tone telling us that we were passing near the outer marker for the ILS approach to Van Nuys. Except for possible practice no one would need that flight aid today; the sky was bright blue and severe clear. We were flying over route 14 in an easterly direction towards the western edge of the Mojave.

Off to my left we soon passed the Agua Dulce Airport. Agua

Dulce had been a fun place. There was a restaurant with good tri

tip sandwiches. The enterprising owner had even built a big

beautiful swimming pool for pilots and their friends and families to

enjoy on those hot southern California summer days. But all that

had been shut down. The airport had been beaten into a mere

shadow of its former self by a small but loud group of dissident

neighbors. Airplanes are still based at Agua Dulce Airport but its

future is in grave doubt. So sad but we motored on.

Directly ahead was the Palmdale Airport. For many years

proponents have championed the cause of Palmdale Airport as a

regional airport to relieve some of the stress ever building upon

Los Angeles International. Recently United Express launched

some limited service from Palmdale. Time will tell whether or not

Palmdale will boom or bust as a regional airport but at least for

now it has come alive. So as one airport is in death throws another nearby seems on it ways towards rebirth. The circle of life plays on.

As we approach Palmdale we are now at 9500 feet and I make a slight course change to the right so we will proceed directly to the Barstow Daggett Airport. Off to my left I briefly study the distant Edwards Air Force base, site of many space shuttle landings and made famous by its depiction in the great movie *The Right Stuff*. Despite being over the rapidly warming rock and sand of the Mojave our flight remains smooth and pleasant. I know that in another hour or so these conditions will no longer exist. The feather soft smoothness we are enjoying now will soon be replaced by ever building violent waves of rapidly rising and descending air beating a frenzied beat upon the aircraft of all airmen who dare to make a midday desert crossing.

At 23 miles east of Palmdale our tranquility is sharply interrupted by the air traffic controller monitoring our progress at Joshua Approach. "Cardinal one three hotel kilo Joshua Approach, traffic twelve o'clock opposite direction eight thousand five hundred, turn five degrees right now vectors for traffic." said the controller. "Wilco (I will comply) three hotel kilo." I said even as I initiated the slight turn. It seemed odd looking out on the vast emptiness of the Mojave to actually have a traffic conflict. But then there is a huge volume of air traffic between Los Angeles and Las Vegas and I was on one of the well worn routes. In only a couple minutes Joshua Approach calls again to inform me that the traffic is no longer a factor and I may resume my own navigation. Neither I nor my eagle eyed daughter ever saw the other airplane, but it surely was there. I just really like having those extra eyes helping me out.

Just below and to my right was the massive 5339 acre Southern California Logistics airport with its two long runways 15050 and 10,000 feet respectively and a 24 hour a day 7 day a week control tower. This virtually impossible to miss landmark grew out of the closed George Air Force Base where the United States Air Force trained many a F4 Phantom jockey before the air base was shut down in 1988. The facility, however, was born in 1941 as the Victorville Army Airfield. Today it serves a wide range of civilian air freight operations as well as elements of the United States military. Even from my lofty perch of 9500 feet it is clearly one huge airfield.

We were rapidly approaching our first destination, the Barstow - Daggett Airport in Daggett, California. I began a gentle descent and as we flew abeam the town of Barstow, California I dialed in the Common Traffic Advisory Frequency of 123.00 and requested an airport advisory. I was informed that there was no other known traffic in the area and the winds were light and variable favoring runway 26. Approaching as we did from the west we descended over some rising terrain to enter the left downwind for runway 26. I descended to 2900 feet MSL (mean sea level) and held that altitude until passing abeam the 26 numbers. Then we reduced power, checked fuel for both tanks, added some flaps, confirmed gear down and welded, fuel boost pump on, landing light on and generally followed the routine for approach to landing announcing our position as we turned from downwind to base and then to final. Full flaps on final, full nose up trim and hold 80 mph until the numbers. All was right with the world. That is until I began my flare and the yoke was blocked by Kari's knees. It seems no matter how hard you try there is always something that can go wrong. Right there and right then my flare was impeded by my sweet young girl who had drawn her legs up to get a better view in preparation for landing. This is one situation no airline pilot will ever encounter. A brief but strong "Kari! Move your legs." solved the problem and the landing was actually quite nice. My utterance was of necessity absent polite niceties. To her ever lasting credit her response was instantaneous and appropriate, another sign of rapidly growing maturity. Still right after all the landing gear was rolling on the runway I did explained to her why daddy omitted the word "please" and why my words were fast and strong. She

nodded her understanding; she didn't pout and she didn't cry. Kari
is growing up quickly. I am thrilled to be taking this trip with her.

After I landed on runway 26 and as I was taxiing towards the fairly
few structures on the field I used my radio to talk with the man at
the FBO and ask him where he wanted me to park. He said "Look
to your right. You will see a twin engine airplane. Park next to it."
That is exactly what I did and as I drew closer to the airplane I
recognized it as one I had seen many times before. It was a
beautiful airplane owned and flown by Mr. & Mrs. Patrick Wayne
Swayze. I had seen it many times at the Van Nuys Airport in Los
Angeles, California. But today, right here and right now, it was
actually parked at the Barstow Daggett Airport in the middle of the
Mojave Desert on the first day of summer.

Patrick Swayze is a former High School athlete, dancer and actor
of substantial accomplishment. His first big break as an actor
came when he played the role of Danny in *GREASE* on Broadway.

Not long after he did what so many before and since have done, he packed his bags and came to Hollywood. After several supporting roles in various TV series in 1983 Patrick Swayze joined a cast that included Tom Cruise, Rob Lowe, Matt Dillon and Emilio Estevez in the classic film *The Outsiders*. His break out film was without doubt his leading role in the smash hit *Dirty Dancing* in 1987. By 1990 his star grew brighter as he joined Demi Moore and Whoopie Goldberg in *Ghost*.

The only time I met Patrick Swayze was in January 2007 when he sat next to me at a memorial service for Frank Kratzer Frank Kratzer was a truly great man, a well accomplished pilot and a dear friend to many including Patrick Swayze and I will dare say even little old me. He had also been flight instructor to Patrick and his wife Lisa. Frank perished on January 12, 2007 in a fiery crash just off the Van Nuys Airport

Today was the first day of summer and there was Patrick Swayze's airplane parked right next to my airplane on the ramp of the

Barstow Daggett Airport and the question immediately popped up: why? I think the answer may well be to remind us that in quiet honor of Captain Frank his friends and protégés fly on.

Aircraft secured and with our bags in hand Kari and I walked toward the gate and the FBO (Fixed Based Operator) office. Still early in the morning the heat was already becoming oppressive. It would peak at 103 degrees this day, the first day of summer.

Standing next to a white several years old Buick was a smiling man. As we approached his smile broadened and he stuck out has hand which I shook as he identified himself as Tom Runyon, proud owner of New Sunrise Auto Sales and the Barstow branch of Rent-a-Wreck. Tom had asked me to call just before I departed Whiteman Airport, which I had done. And as promised he was waiting for us on arrival at the Barstow – Daggett Airport. We placed our bags in his car and went inside the small FBO building and met Ron Jr. of Daggett Aviation. Ron Jr. cheerfully told us that we had just parked next to Patrick Swayze's airplane and how

the fabulous Barstow – Daggett airport was frequently visited by

Hollywood celebrities including many visits by Angelina Jolie.

Our $2.50 overnight tie down fee having been duly paid and

recorded we bid farewell to Ron Jr. and headed back out into the

heat to the white Buick from Rent-a-Wreck.

On the map the distance between the Barstow – Daggett Airport

and the town of Barstow, California is only about a half an inch.

In the car it is more like 10 miles. As we drove past the United

States Marine Corps logistics base, that event became the catalyst

bringing forth the information that both Tom Runyon and I had

served in the Corps. Well a hardy *Semper Fi!* Tom had been a

Marine Corps MP and hadn't much cared for the job. The Marine

Corps is really funny that way. There are literally hundreds of

thousands of former Marines, many of whom were not all that

pleased with their work in the Corps but who nevertheless have

great pride in their Marine Corps service. I can only imagine that the Marines stationed at the logistics facility in Barstow are mostly

very displeased with their duty station. No matter how important

the job may be to the overall performance of the mission of the

United States Marine Corps, there just is not much Glory in

counting military supplies in triple digit temperatures in the middle

of the Mojave Desert. *Ou Rah!*

Back at his office we completed the paperwork necessary for

renting the old white Buick and learned that Tom Runyon was a

super Baltimore Orioles and Cal Ripken fan.   He also once made

an unsuccessful bid for the Barstow city council. He was nothing

if not conversational and a rather interesting guy to discover in

Barstow, California. We took our paperwork and some driving

directions and our day of ground exploration began.

We drove first to the Barstow train station and Harvey House

museum for a look around. There was something about the

architecture of those old buildings that touched old memories of train stations back in the Midwest where I grew up. There is also a great deal of railroad activity in Barstow and we happened upon two train enthusiasts very much enjoying the sights and sounds. Their look of utter contentment and deep happiness with the railroad environment was identical to what I have seen often in the eyes of pilots hanging around any airport.

A common yet critical condition had struck Kari. She was hungry. So off we went to Peggy Sue's Nifty Fifties Diner in nearby Yermo, California. Peggy Sue's Diner is a true classic; originally built in 1954 it was extensively refurbished in 1987. It is a living museum of American 1950's pop culture that happily also continues to serve generous portions of very tasty and standard American food. Expect great hamburgers, steaks, chili and soup. Don't even think about haute cuisine. Do think of and enjoy listening to Elvis Presley, Buddy Holly, Ritchie Valens and Ricky Nelson. Forget about 50 Cent, Snoop Dog and Christina Aguilera. It is a true time machine and both Kari and I thoroughly enjoyed the trip back in time. For her it was all new and for me it was all memories. Now someday it will be a fond memory for my daughter Kari too. Just how long she will remember the huge piece of strawberry rhubarb pie a la mode is debatable, but the over all experience will no doubt last her lifetime.

Well fed our next stop was the fabulous Calico Ghost Town conveniently located right on Ghost Town Road not far from Peggy Sue's Diner. Most people are at least somewhat familiar with the fabled California gold rush, but there was also a California silver rush that had Calico as its epicenter. Calico was officially born in March of 1881 to support the burgeoning in flow of silver miners to the area. At its peak Calico and nearby environs had a population of several thousand people with Calico itself claiming about 1200 residents, 22 saloons and 500 silver mines. In the mid 1890's the silver market crumbled and with it the backbone of Calico. By 1907, a mere 16 years after its official establishment

Calico was completely abandoned. Last of its original inhabitants, Mrs. Lucy Bell Lane died in the 1960's. Her original home can still been visited today in Calico where it now serves as a museum.

Important history shall not be denied, however, so in 1951 entrepreneur and Knott's Berry Farm founder Walter Knott bought the whole town and began the task of restoring it. Approximately one third of the structures that exist in Calico today are refurbished original structures. Many others are built upon original foundations. Overall it is a great tribute to the original residents of Calico and the important role they played in the development of the western United States. It is also a great deal of fun to visit.

In 1966, Walter Knott donated Calico to the County of San Bernardino, California and it became a county park. As can be expected some folks believe that the ghosts of the early miners continue to haunt the town. That may or may not be true. What is true is that today Calico hosts thousands of visitors from all over the world every day. Staged gun fights, characters dressed in period clothing, numerous special events and several fascinating shops, displays and exhibits entertain and inform the guests. Kari and I walked the length of the town visiting most if not all of the shops and exhibits. We also took a ride on the small narrow gauge railroad, the Calico & Odessa Railroad that circles the area while historical locations and events are pointed out.

Our final activity at Calico was a visit of the Maggie Mine. It is a fairly short walking tour within a once operating mine. Immediately upon entry to your left is an impressive display of some of the indigenous mineralization in the Calico area. A brief recorded lecture and the use of a black light makes for a highly informative and captivating presentation. Other displays show various early mining operations and the living and working conditions of the Calico miners. But frankly the most compelling reason for the Maggie Mine tour is that within the walls of the mine the temperature stays right around 69 degrees even when it is triple digits outside. So fun and informative yes, but cool and refreshing YES!

CALICO GHOST TOWN, YERMO, CALIFORNIA

Returning to our Rent-a-Wreck Buick with more than 112000 miles on the odometer we were very happy to find that its air conditioner worked splendidly. One of the things I had hoped to accomplish on this adventure was a little rock hunting, and what better place than the Calico mountains. So upon exiting the Calico Ghost Town Park we drove first east and then south on Calico Road for about 2 miles to Mule Canyon Road. Mule Canyon Road is rocky and fairly narrow but it was clearly leading us in a northerly direction towards what seemed like excellent rock hunting opportunities. But alas as we bumped along on a road I am sure the owner of the vehicle would prefer we not be on I made a mistake fatal to this rock hunting expedition. I began discussing with Kari critters such as scorpions and rattlesnakes and how they inhabited areas like the very one we were in. I am absolutely certain that Kari will enjoy a very successful life because she exhibits an uncanny ability for real critical thinking. This day her thinking went something like this. "Let's see now, we have triple digit heat, a very rough trail, possible scorpions and rattlesnakes, or a cool swimming pool, cold drinks and food back at the hotel." Her decision was swift and clear. "Dad, let's go to the hotel now" said the obviously brilliant Kari.

So we rumbled back and eventually rejoined actual pavement. We eventually came upon a road which, had we turned to our right rather than to our left, would have taken us to nearby Fort Irwin. Hey now that is impressive, a Fort named after us – wow! Well not actually. Nevertheless Fort Irwin is used extensively and appropriately enough for training our troops for desert warfare. Here was yet another selling point for Navy recruiters. The age old Navy slogan is "Join the Navy and see the world." The updated version reads: "Join the Navy and avoid desert warfare." Then again is months on end submerged in a submarine really all that much better? It is all perspective.

Kari and I had a quick and unmemorable meal before she spent some refreshing time in the swimming pool while I concurrently watched her and went over our flight plan for the next day. We had enjoyed a very active first day starting with our take off from the Whiteman Airport in Los Angeles, California, a one hundred mile flight mostly over the Mojave Desert, our landing at the Barstow – Daggett Airport and our ground tours to the Harvey House, Peggy Sue's Nifty Fifties Diner, the Calico Ghost Town, some almost rock hunting and a nice swim. Truly it had been a great start to a great adventure and now it was time to rest before continuing on. Tomorrow would bring more flying, to Kingman, Arizona, but less in things entertaining for both parent and child. Still it was all part of the total trip. Soon both Kari and I were asleep, pleasantly exhausted from a very exciting and eventful day. Tomorrow, day two, was only hours away.

Day Two

W e got up early as planned, about 5:45 AM and quickly packed our clothes. I tossed our bags in the trunk of our Rent-a-Wreck Buick and strolled into the motel lobby to check out and eat our complimentary "Continental Breakfast." There were only two or perhaps three other folks up and running at that hour which worked out just fine because the available area was rather small. Minimally fed but well rested we set off back to Rent-a-Wreck to return our rented car and be driven back to the Barstow – Daggett Airport. True to his word Tom Runyon was waiting for us at his place of business bright and early. We finished up our paper work and quickly left for the airport. Yeah the car was old with almost as much mileage as me. But the price was right and the service provided by Tom

30

Runyon was excellent. Now let me explain more fully our sense of urgency.

We were flying over mainly desert and some mountains on our trip. Desert and mountains are mostly rock and dirt or sand. Rock and sand reflect heat much more vigorously than green grass or blue water for example. As the sun rises the heat reflecting off of the rock and sand increases in intensity. As we all know hot air rises. So as the temperature increases so does the vigor with which the hot air lifts skyward thus creating some truly awesome turbulence. By midday flying in a small personal airplane over such terrain can be down right miserable. My daughter is no fan of misery and neither am I. So to prevent exposure to such unpleasant flying conditions we elected to depart very early each day of our trip. It mainly worked and worked well.

Back at the airport Kari and I bid farewell to Tom Runyon and carried our bags passed the gate, on to the ramp and to our airplane. We opened the doors to the airplane and placed the bags inside making sure to secure them. I began walking around the airplane checking fuel quantity and condition as well as testing all flight controls and control surfaces to make certain that they were free and clear and absent any visible damage. I looked at the tires checking for inflation and the absence of any significant wear, cuts or abrasions. I checked the oil for quantity and condition and the radio antennas to make sure they were all present and accounted for and securely attached. Kari busied herself detaching the tie down chains. The aircraft appeared to be airworthy. The sky was totally void of any visible moisture and the wind was negligible. There being no clear reason to do otherwise I made one last look around the aircraft to assure Kari had done her job, which she had, and then climbed aboard and prepared for departure.

I unfolded my chart, a CG-18 World Aeronautical Chart,

reconfirmed my printed flight plan which was pretty simple

reading DAG – IGM heading 064 degrees. Next I turned on the

Garmin GPS and activated the Daggett to Kingman routing. I

looked at Kari making sure that her door and seatbelt were

securely fastened which they were. I asked "Are you ready Kari?"

to which she immediately replied "roger." This kid is going to

become a pilot yet I thought. I primed the engine, set the brake,

cracked the throttle, set the mixture slightly lean due to the field

elevation, turned on the master switch and bellowed "CLEAR" just

before turning the key to start.   The engine fired up immediately

without hesitation and quickly settled into a nice smooth idle at

1000 RPM.

The next task was to set up our radios. The communication

frequency remained as we had left it on 123.00 MHz. I dialed in

the ASOS frequency for Kingman, it being 119.275 MHz. As we

got closer to Kingman I would able to hear broadcasts of the current weather conditions. The sky was clear literally for hundreds of miles but I would want to know the altimeter setting, wind speed and direction and density altitude for Kingman prior to arrival. Even though we had a great GPS unit and a known heading it had been my experience a few times on past trips in and out of the Kingman area that as the aircraft approached the Colorado River the GPS would lose all satellite reception. Not just weak signals mind you but zero reception. This has to be a deliberate action by our military. Maybe it relates to somewhat nearby Nellis Air Force Base or maybe even the not too far away legendary Area 51, but whatever the cause having a good back up to the GPS was essential to safe navigation on this portion of the trip. That being the case I dialed in the Goffs VOR at 114.4 MHz and the Kingman VOR at 108.8 MHz. For the non aviator reader a VOR (Very High Frequency Omni directional Radio Range) is an old but effective navigation aid. Essentially all one needs to do is dial up the frequency of the closest VOR ahead (or behind), turn the omni bearing selector until the needle stays in the center and an indicator points up or down indicating whether you are flying to or from the station and just fly there with the needle centered. Yes this is an over simplification but I think it conveys the basic idea. Turn it on, tune it in, center the needle and fly there. Pretty cool actually and the VOR works when the GPS does not for whatever reason except total power failure when it all quits. Of course flying the known heading, checking the ground references depicted on our chart and making corrections as necessary for the wind will also get you there. There is also a venerable and proven navigation technique known as dead reckoning when you factor in speed, time and distance calculations. All of this had been calculated, planned, plotted and dialed in and we were ready to go navigationally speaking.

Given our known heading of 064 degrees and further considering that there was essentially no wind at that moment at the Barstow –

Daggett Airport Kari and I began our taxi to runway 08. As we headed out another pilot in a Piper Cherokee was announcing his arrival for runway 26. Since our take off would take us directly at the arriving aircraft we took our time taxing out doing the necessary run-up procedures along the way. Everything checked out, all gauges were in the green and the world was at peace, at least within the cockpit of Cessna Cardinal 13 Hotel Kilo. Soon the arriving traffic announced that he was down and clear. We then made our own announcement advising any traffic in or near the Barstow Daggett airport that Cardinal 13 Hotel Kilo was about to take runway 08 for an immediate straight out (more or less) departure. We placed the flaps at 10 degrees, confirmed that the cowl flaps were open and that our fuel selector was on both tanks. All gauges were in the green; all gyro instruments were performing as advertised and we were once again for the second time in about 24 hours ready for take off. The propeller control was set full forward, the mixture slightly leaned, carburetor heat was off and I eased the throttle all the way forward. The airplane quickly picked up speed and I gradually increased pressure on the right rudder to keep the aircraft on the runway centerline. Once again we very quickly lifted gently into the sky heading almost directly at the rising sun.

I already mentioned how making flights over the desert in the early morning helps considerably in assuring a smooth ride. So does flying as high as possible considering the conditions and aircraft performance. This day that meant we would climb to an indicated altitude of 11,500 feet MSL (above mean sea level). The Cessna Cardinal is in my opinion and the opinion of many others absolutely without question the most comfortable single engine airplane ever built by Cessna or pretty much anyone else for that matter. And the Cardinal does fly a bit faster than any of the Cessna 172's or Piper Cherokee's. That is the good news. The bad news is that Cardinal's are notorious for relatively slow and hot climbs. That is to say that for whatever reason, cowl design most likely, the engine tends to get rather hot in an extended climb and especially on a hot day like this day. The slow part comes from two factors. One is that as with all non turbo charged reciprocating (piston –v- jet) engines with every foot of altitude engine efficiency declines due to steadily dropping air pressure. Airplane engines need to breathe much like people. And much like people as altitude increases the ability to perform that necessary task is reduced. But this is not an aeronautical engineering book so just keep in mind as the plane goes up engine performance gradually but significantly goes down. Also adding to the total time to cruise altitude is the fact that to keep safe it s frequently required to step climb a Cardinal. To step climb one merely levels off every couple thousand feet to allow the engine to cool down a bit before continuing the climb. That is exactly the procedure I adopted this warm summer day over the Mojave Desert.

As we reached 7500 I leveled off for a few minutes to allow the engine to cool. I looked at the gauges and saw that both the Exhaust Gas Temperature gauge and the Cylinder Head Temperature gauge were well within parameters, but that the oil temperature gauge was showing signs of excess engine heating. After a few minutes of level flight with the cowl flaps still in the open position I could see the oil temperature begin to ease so I added power and pitched up once again.

Our next plateau was at 9500 feet where I once again leveled off for a few more minutes. The oil temperature had gotten even higher than before but it was still in the green. After about 5 to 10 minutes of level flight I pitched up for our last climb to 11,500 feet. Given the more rarified air at this altitude engine performance was noticeably less and the climb took longer than the previous climbs. By the time we reached 11,500 feet the oil temperature had risen to just below the red line. It was still in the green, but it was I admit nipping at the heels of that red line. Clearly we were done climbing, I trimmed for level flight and after a few minutes when I saw the oil temperature begin to cool I asked Kari to close the cowl flaps. She gave me one of those "Huh?" looks. I smiled back at her and then pointed out the cowl flap lever on the lower center pedestal. At first she could not get it to go down. So I told her that she needed to first pull it slightly toward her and then push down. She did that and now the cowl flaps were closed. The cowl flaps were closed, we were trimmed for level flight, power was set, all the gauges were in the green and we were heading in the right direction. One more great day in the annals of aviation was underway.

The terrain below was about as barren and foreboding as it gets, at least in California. Between the Barstow Daggett Airport and the Colorado River it really mostly resembles moonscape. Well we did cross over Kelso, California yet another California mining town turned ghost town, but there wasn't much of anything to see from our perch about two miles above. Much more exciting than Kelso below us was the loss of GPS Satellite signals from above us. As predicted by the time we reached Kelso our GPS had become useless. I am convinced this is no accident. I have even heard airline crews speak of the same phenomenon in this particular area in the sky. There absolutely positively must be some military installation or activity in the area that our military does not want to be precisely honed in on. But what and where? I doubt I will ever know. The good news is that we were receiving a very strong signal from the Goffs VOR just ahead to our east.

Upon reaching the Goffs VOR we turned slightly to our right for a direct path to the Kingman, Arizona Airport. Out my left window about 15 miles to the north I could see the small town of Searchlight, Nevada. Searchlight, Nevada, much like Calico, California and Kelso, California was born of mining. In 1907

Searchlight, Nevada reached the staggering population of about 5000 people, much more than Las Vegas at that time. By 1927 the quantity and quality of gold ore coming from Searchlight, Nevada had dropped dramatically as had the population to only about 50 folks still hanging in there. Today it boasts a hotel casino and a population of about 2000 citizens. One of the two United States Senators from the Great State of Nevada, Harry Reid was born in Searchlight, Nevada. But to me most importantly about four, or was it five years earlier I had flown to Searchlight Nevada with Kari's older sister Kimberly. It was my birthday celebration and after we landed at the tiny and essentially barren Searchlight, Nevada airport she presented me with my birthday gift, a great big huge book entitled *USMC A Complete History*. I cherish the book, of course, but even more I cherish the flight with her that wonderful day. After her gift presentation we flew on to nearby Bullhead City, Arizona and then crossed the Colorado River into Laughlin, Nevada for a nice lunch at the Colorado Belle. After lunch we fought significant turbulence to Blythe, California and then eventually back home to the Whiteman Airport. It was rocky but fun and I will remember that day fondly to my last breath. But that was then and this is now.

Kari's beautiful eyes lit up with joy as she pointed out her window and announced: "Dad look, a big building on the river!" Sure enough we were rapidly coming up on Laughlin, Nevada and Kari's first glimpse of the Colorado River. "Yes dear, that is Laughlin, Nevada and the Colorado River. We will soon be in Kingman, Arizona" I intoned. She seemed very pleased with that knowledge. She is a great travel companion and a good co pilot but she was not yet fully at ease with the whole flying experience. So being close to a scheduled landing was a very pleasing thought to her. We motored on crossing the river and drawing ever closer to Kingman, Arizona.

I dialed in the Kingman Unicom frequency of 122.8 MHz on my com one radio and then punched in the preselected ASOS frequency of 119.275 on my com two radio. *Viola!* We had contact with Kingman. The wind was favoring runway 21 and from the radio chatter it was clear that other aircraft were using runway 21 so that would be our runway on arrival. With both the town and the airport coming into view on the horizon I reduced power and pitched slightly down beginning a gradual descent.

On my first visit to Kingman, Arizona I was told by a local resident that the way Kingman was established was as a group of settlers moved west they stopped at the spot that was to become Kingman and promised to continue on once the wind calmed down. Steadily their numbers grew and the population of Kingman, Arizona continues to grow to this day.

The actual history of what became Kingman, Arizona is even more interesting than the wind story. In 1857 the United States Army dispatched Lieutenant Edward F. Beale to survey wagon trails along the 35th parallel. It was in the month of October of that year that Lt. Beale and his band of men reached what has become Kingman, Arizona. However, unlike the image portrayed in the venerable "Western" movies their mode of transportation was not gallant horses. Rather Lt. Beale was the leader of a caravan of camels. While there was certainly mining activity in the area Kingman, Arizona did not grow so much out of the mining activity as it did from the arrival of the railroad. Kingman, Arizona was and is a railroad town.

In 1880 Lewis Kingman surveyed the railroad right of way that ran between Needles, California and Albuquerque, New Mexico and within a mere three years the tracks of Atlantic and Pacific Railroad had been laid. In the course of this process Beale Springs became Kingman. With the railroad in place Kingman, Arizona grew rapidly from a population of about 300 in 1890 to approximately 500 in 1900. Today the greater Kingman, Arizona area claims a population of about 40,000 people.

As a life long pilot I was, of course, fascinated to learn that the first airport was laid out by none other than Charles Lindberg. As happened to so many airports in America during World War Two the Kingman Army Air Field was established in 1942 and it is that air field that continues to serve Kingman, Arizona to this very day. Near the small terminal at the Kingman airport stands the original control tower used by the Army Air Corps during the war. Today there are no air traffic control facilities at the Kingman, Arizona airport.

As we swept gracefully over southwest end of the air field we increased our rate of descent slightly and went a little beyond the airport to set up for a 45 degree entry into the down wind for runway 21. I heard another airplane in bound from the east and heading for a landing on runway 17 at Kingman. From his position reports it appeared that he would be on the ground well ahead of us but nevertheless I began slowing our airplane to assure a wide margin. We turned our Cardinal to a heading of 030 degrees as we reached and held the altitude of 4450 feet MSL and flew north east parallel to the runway below us to our left. We announced our position on the left downwind for runway 21 Kingman. Quickly it was time to descend further and set up for landing at the Kingman, Arizona airport. Proper power adjustments, flap settings and radio calls were made and we lined up nicely for the center line on runway 21. At this point I asked Kari to please open the cowl flaps. Now she immediately performed the task quickly and correctly and with a big happy smile. Cowl flap operation had just been included in her list of co pilot duties.

The landing, while not a greaser, was nevertheless satisfactory to everyone except my most severe critic who pronounced it not so good. "That was kind of a rough one dad" said Kari with a twinkle in her eye and pretty smile on her lips. She absolutely does not subscribe to that old pilots adage that any landing you walk away from is a good one. She holds me to a much higher standard. Oh well. As we taxied off of the runway she did, however, make one very important observation that began as a question. "Daddy" she asked as she pointed to the oil temperature gauge to her left, "Is that supposed to be red?" "Heck no!" I replied and then I asked: "Why do you ask?" "Well daddy because back there when were climbing it looked red to me" she said adding "But once we leveled off it became green again." I was deeply impressed at how this still young girl had made a very important observation of a critical flight condition. Oil temperature indications in the red are absolutely not a good thing and I said so to Kari. I also complimented her on her keen observation. But I did point out to her that should she make any other observations of that sort it would be best to tell me right away and not to wait until we got on the ground. I had been keeping a sharp eye on that gauge and while it did get close to the red line it never passed into it. Still her observation was significant and we added gauge monitoring and condition reporting to her list of co pilot duties. A lot of licensed pilots could easily overlook that critical measurement. Kari caught it and kept vigilance on all the gauges for the rest of the trip.

I taxied over to what had been an FBO on my last visit to Kingman. It is very distinctive with a huge three bladed propeller arching over its entrance. After engine shut down Kari and I tied down the airplane, secured the control lock, placed the pitot tube cover on the pitot tube and engine cowling cover in its proper place and then removed our bags and walked into the building. A nice young lady greeted us and I immediately volunteered that we needed fuel and that we would be there for the night. She immediately replied that the FBO was no longer the occupant of this facility but rather we were now standing in the facility of the Airport Authority. Holy cow! The Kingman, Arizona Airport Authority. This place really was trying hard to be in the big league. Of course part of such progress is money so we dutifully paid the previously not required $5.00 over night ramp fee and made arrangements for fuel to be delivered to our airplane. I then asked if they might be able to give us a ride to the other end of the field and Sheble Aviation, a very interesting flight training company and a big reason for us being in Kingman, Arizona on this 22nd day of June. Indeed transportation arrangements were quickly made and Kari and I were driven to Sheble to meet my good friend Darren Baird who had arrived the previous night to begin further training towards earning his instrument flight rating from Sheble.

Sheble Aviation has been around for many years. Exactly how many I can not say nor am I sufficiently intrigued to research that detail, but it has been around for many years. It was established I believe by Joseph Sheble Senior who continues to serve the business as both an instructor and FAA Designated Pilot Examiner. The day to day operational chores passed some time ago to Joseph Sheble Junior and his wife Valerie. Per their advertising their forte is "accelerated" flight training. They advertise fairly heavily in several aviation publications and indeed have "graduated" many pilots with ratings from Private Pilot up to and including Airline Transport Pilot. The essence of their appeal is that you can achieve almost any particular license or rating quickly and almost certainly with them for one set fee. I have never heard of them ever being accused of focusing on quality. Many of their customers leave happy having received their desired rating within the prescribed time and for the set fee. Others leave frustrated and

51

angry either with or without their desired license or rating. Sheble has long been a controversial operation but they do seem to deliver ratings on time and as agreed. For this reason I had actually recommended my friend Darren Baird to go the Sheble for his instrument rating. I explained to Darren that it is indeed possible to receive an instrument rating without being truly instrument competent. I further explained that Sheble did seem to deliver as promised and that by getting his rating there he could get passed the bureaucratic element and continue to work on his advanced skills after the fact. Darren and I share at least one common personality trait, we both tend to be very jealous of our time. For this reason the Sheble program appealed to him. For this reason he also became disenchanted.

To my eyes nothing had greatly changed in the Sheble facility. Their ramp was still across a road from the airport proper creating a rare opportunity for pilots to actually taxi on a road on their way to the airport. Inside the dominant feature is a fairly large combined kitchen and lounge area. Further within the facility is a training room an office or two, a restroom and a Jacuzzi type device that I am convinced is where they conduct the seaplane rating training. In the unisex bathroom there is an interesting sign admonishing instructors and students alike to make the application of deodorant a mandatory element of their preflight procedures. Well it is indeed hot in the desert and very close quarters in all general aviation aircraft.

Standing in the lounge/kitchen area was a somewhat haggard looking Darren. With more than a twinge of irritation in his voice he quickly informed me that despite being told to be at the facility no later than 8:00 AM he had no flying scheduled for this day. He was scheduled for a two hour ground session at 2:00 PM several hours hence. So off we went to get settled in our hotel and then grab a bite to eat.

Immediately upon arriving at the lobby of the hotel Kari spotted the swimming pool. Finally she had a reason, arguably the only reason from her perspective, for being here. In keeping with the general aura of frustration for the day we were not yet able to check in to our hotel room so we stowed our bags in Darren's room and headed out to lunch.

Motivated mainly be ease and convenience we went to a family style restaurant nearby and had a decent lunch. Over lunch Darren related his frustrations over what he deemed an egregious waste of his time and we discussed options. When we got back to the airport and Sheble Darren was summoned into what was being called a two hour ground instruction session. Kari found a computer terminal and immediately entertained herself with some on line games. I walked over and picked up my fuel receipt and toyed with the idea of using Darren's car for some touring. That idea was rejected and honestly it turned out to be a rather boring day for both father and daughter. But we put a good spin on it and simply called this day a day of rest.

With his ground instruction done some three, not two but three hours later Darren, Kari and I headed off for dinner. We each enjoyed a decent steak at the Kingman Company Steal House before returning to the hotel and another swimming session for Kari. On our way back to our hotel we did do at least a driving tour inevitably on sections of the Mother Road, the fabled Route 66 and eventually of Historic Downtown Kingman. It is quaint and it does have a bit of an old west flavor. However we missed the locomotive park, the powerhouse and the hiking trails that more or less round out the main tourist attractions of Kingman, Arizona. Rather we turned in early in preparation for what promised to be a much busier, more fun and more active day starting early the next morning.

Day Three

(Kingman Airport, AZ –to- Grand Canyon Airport, AZ)

100 NM 1.1 Hours

For the next several days we were going to be flying in high terrain country. Kingman Airport sat at the relatively low elevation of a mere 3449 feet MSL. Our destination airport, however, Grand Canyon National Park Airport had a rather impressive elevation of 6609 feet MSL. But then absolutely everything about Grand Canyon is impressive, even planning to get there by airplane is impressive. For instance the Grand Canyon National Park actually has its very own VFR (visual flight rules) Aeronautical Chart. One side of the chart is for general aviation operations. That side was for us. The other side is specifically for Air Tour Operations and that was absolutely not us.

So as had already become our habit we rose early and had a quick but pleasant light breakfast before being driven to the Kingman Airport for the start of this day's adventure. Darren dropped us off at our airplane and then headed off to Sheble to see what they had planned for him this day. Kari and I had finished all of the pre start pre flight activity and we were just about ready to secure the doors and start the engine when Darren came steaming back in a rage. "I'm not even on the schedule for today" he sputtered. We very quickly exchanged some words of condolence and discussed some options but we really had to get going. I did not want to tackle a 6609 foot elevation in triple digit heat. Darren completely understood and bid us farewell promising to keep in touch as his situation played out that day.

Doors locked and seat belts securely fastened I noticed that Kari automatically confirmed that the cowl flaps were open as I started the engine. Once again good old Cardinal one three hotel kilo

57

came to life immediately. While I did feel bad for Darren I could sense already that this was going to be a great day for Kari and me. The winds were still light but favoring runway 3 so off we went for a runway 3 departure all the while both looking and listening for traffic. When all seemed clear we took the runway, added power and at the appropriate moment took off.

While our runway heading was close to our on course heading I never the less flew for a short while on the down wind while maintaining a climb. By the time we turned upwind and got established on the on course heading we were at least 1500 feet above the pattern altitude for the Kingman Airport. The reason I did this was partially because we had experienced a very hot, but still within parameters, engine inbound yesterday and I wanted to see if the engine warmed up at an expected and normal rate today which it did. Had I seen any hint of an over heating problem I could easily have landed back at Kingman even in the highly unlikely event of a catastrophic engine failure. If, however, I immediately turned on to our on course heading and something went wrong the landing options would have been much more frightening. I also wanted to make sure we had abundant time to reach an altitude well above what was up ahead. But truthfully I doubt I would have taken this precaution were it not for the very precious living cargo sitting directly to my right. It was my solemn duty to take every measure to assure that Kari had an experience that was comfortable, fun, informative and most of all safe. Consequently we flew a wee bit longer in a box pattern on our way out of Kingman, Arizona.

Fortunately my GPS was working well and stayed working well for the entire trip. Still as a matter of extra prudence I dialed in the Peach Springs VOR on 112.00 MHz and identified the station. That would be our primary navigation aid and would get the job done in the event the GPS once again went out.

It was early but still after 8:00 AM as we flew serenely along on our way to the Grand Canyon. I was surprised by the total absence of radio chatter along this route. True, the Kingman to Grand Canyon routing was probably not flown nearly as much as other options and routings, but it was still surprising and pleasant. The sky in every direction was also flawlessly clear. Consequently very soon after we reached our cruising altitude of 11,500 feet MSL we could see parts of the rapidly approaching Grand Canyon. Kari completed her assigned task of closing the cowl flaps as we leveled off, and then Kari double checked our engine gauges before riveting her attention of the rapidly changing topography below and ahead.

As we got ever closer to our destination there was an amazing clear line of demarcation between barren desert brown and deep green from a forest of Ponderosa pine.

My auditory silence was broken with the at first scratchy and intermittent and then steady and clear broadcasts of the Grand Canyon National Park airport ATIS (Automated Terminal Information Service) on 124.3 MHz. The wind was light, at or below 5 knots and favoring runway 21. Great! Like most high altitude airports Grand Canyon National Park airport had a reputation of having often strong and gusting winds. That would be the condition today but not until well after we had landed and tied down our airplane. Next I could hear conversations between the tower and other aircraft on 119.00 MHz. And then amidst the magnificent Ponderosa pines we saw the airport. I reported my position to the tower and we were cleared for right traffic for runway 21 and told to report downwind. "Wilco, Cardinal 3 hotel kilo" I replied and then we reduced power and pitched down aiming for a point about one mile to our left of the runway.

The entire trip of just under 100 nautical miles had been as smooth as silk. Ahead of us was a forest of pine and just beyond it was the absolutely stunning Grand Canyon. It was the first time either one of us had ever seen this amazing wonder. It played with my senses and taunted me to abandon my flying chores but reluctantly I stayed steady on the task at hand. Now we were over the pine trees and still descending with the forest steadily gaining detail. At exactly 7500 MSL but slightly less than 900 feet above the ground I took a heading of 030 degrees and just one mile to the west of the field, pushed the push to talk switch and said "Grand Canyon tower, Cardinal one three hotel kilo, right down wind runway two one." Immediately the controller responded with "Cardinal one three hotel kilo cleared to land runway two one." Now the canyon itself had slid below my line of sight. Replacing it was a slight rise upon which stood many large Ponderosa pine trees just begging me to adorn them with my airplane as a macabre Christmas tree ornament. They now had my full attention. Given my view of things I shortened my approach somewhat making my turn to base and then final sooner than I might have done without all of the pretty wood in front of me. The 150 foot wide 9000 foot long runway was an easy target and we settled down right after the numbers with gentleness appropriate to the venue. Dang this was one beautiful place. We taxied off and parked the airplane. Kari and I got out and before starting our usual chores we both just stood there breathing in the lightly pine scented, comfortably warm, arid and remarkably fresh mountain air. Well actually I think we were on a high mesa and not precisely a mountain but it had the same effect and it was deeply pleasant.

You would think that being located at a true world class tourist destination and literally less than 2 miles from a small but vibrant airport with numerous commercial as well as private flights every day there would be some kind of shuttle service between the airport and the handful of local hotels. That was, however, absolutely almost violently not the case at the Grand Canyon

National Park Airport nor at the Red Feather Lodge where we had reserved a room. Being as most of them are friendly and accommodating folks, the good people at the FBO did agree and in fact did give us a ride the one and one half miles to our hotel. Now all we had to do was figure out how we were going to get back to the airplane tomorrow morning. That proved a far more daunting task than I could at first imagine. But first we are here to see the Grand Canyon and see the Grand Canyon we shall.

Basically I hate organized tours. I always have. I have been blessed with the opportunity to have literally traveled the world visiting every continent but Australia and Antarctica. I hope to get to Australia soon and despite the movies *Happy Feet* and *Surfs Up* I have no driving interest in Antarctica. In all these years of travel I only once before resorted to using a group tour service. Today, however, my penchant for serendipity needed as a practical matter to be suspended. We had no transportation of our own and rental cars were for some odd reason unavailable. Walking to the rim was at least 16 miles round trip and had we done that we would have seen but one very small part of one truly huge canyon.

Nope we needed to take an organized commercial tour like it or not. The problem was with whom? The answer, whomsoever we could first find to take us. One of the hotel staff, Nancy Halstead, took instantly to the task one after another calling all of the known local tour companies and getting the same response every where. "Sorry, but we are filled up for the day. Oh oh! Had I really dropped the ball? Had I flown my daughter all the way to the Grand Canyon only to never actually see it, at least not from the ground? I was determined not to let her or me for that matter, down. Somehow we would get there even if it meant hiring a very expensive taxi cab or even worse, paying another pilot to fly us around because this pilot had been too dumb to plan adequately ahead. Maybe they would have given me a dumb pilot's discount.

These thoughts and others raced through my head as we headed back to our room to drop our bags and find a solution. By the time we got back to the hotel lobby Nancy Halstead had risen in my mind to near goddess status; she had booked us on a tour and we would be leaving in about 20 minutes. Against all odds and in the face of repeated rejection Nancy had come though. Bless her.

It was about 30 minutes later when we got our first ground level look at the Grand Canyon. It is truly breath taking. A vast abyss rimmed with layer upon layer of mostly red and brown sedimentary rock a mile deep. It is majestic like no other natural monument I had ever seen on this earth. It is truly and totally WOW! Numbers don't tell it all and the photo that follows is but a tiny glimpse. Yet just think about this. The Grand Canyon is an area of 1.2 million acres. That is bigger the Bill Gates house, much bigger. It runs 277 miles and averages a depth of 4000 feet but reaches 6000 feet at its deepest and 15 miles across at it's widest. The Grand Canyon National Park contains several ecosystems including three of the four desert systems. It is literally millions of years old and a super paleontological, geological, archeological and biological resource wonder. But first and foremost to regular people it is a mind blowing humbling stunning sight to behold.

GRAND CANYON, ARIZONA

Our intrepid tour guide told us that most people actually spend an average of about 8 minutes in the Grand Canyon National Park, stopping solely at the first observation point inside the gate. To me that is close to going to the Metropolitan Museum of Art and stopping only in the bathroom to view the graffiti and then leaving. We Homo sapiens are often rather weird.   Our first stop was a few miles beyond the common initial viewing area and once there we were treated to some general information about the Grand Canyon. Honestly, were I on a scientific expedition perhaps I would have been more interested, but as a common sightseer. Mother Nature had clearly done a much better job of getting my attention and Kari's attention than any guide was ever going to get.

We were then invited to walk along a well manicured path allowing for a bit more than one and one half miles to the El Tovar Hotel where our tour guide would rejoin us and we would enjoy a bite to eat. For more than 25 minutes Kari and I were immersed in overwhelming natural beauty, majesty and serenity. The scene before us was constantly changing. We saw birds we had never seen before. Almost constantly below us was a thin sliver that was in fact the raging Colorado River that was both deep and wide but from where we stood was little more than a strand of hair. The air was almost painfully fresh with a steady hint of pine and sage and juniper, warm and soothing. Why I wondered had I denied myself this experience for 62 years? Pleased I was that I had delivered this to my daughter Kari in her 11th year. Confident I was that she would carry the memory of this experience with her for the rest of her life on earth. Determined I became to assure that both my wife Nenita and my daughter Kimberly would be brought here as well.

Soon we saw three buildings just ahead on our trail. That was our assigned rallying point and we were the first of our group to arrive. At first there was a building on our left that was a gift/souvenir/trinket shop. That did not appeal to us so we ambled on. Directly to our front was the majestic El Tovar Lodge and to our right was the intriguing Hopi house. The Hopi House had been the work product of one of America's first women architects Mary Colter born in Pittsburgh, Pennsylvania April 4, 1869.

In her youth Mary Colter moved steadily westward with her family from Pennsylvania to Minnesota to Colorado and then Texas. She eventually made it to San Francisco, California where she studied at the California School of Design. In 1901 she took a job with the Fred Harvey Company of national Harvey House fame. She rapidly expanded her career from an interior designer to a highly regarded architect. Keep in mind that this amazing woman accomplished all of this at a time in our history when women were still striving to get the right to vote. Her positive approach to life and her career achievements reminded me very much of my late great aunt Merle Irwin who during a similar time frame taught in rural one room school houses in Illinois, earned her Masters

Degree at the University of Chicago and went on to become a very powerful force in public education. Different venues and professions, but they shared an equal commitment to themselves and their success. Not once were they reported to sing protest songs, join marches or burn bras. They just went and did it. I am confident that Kari will learn and benefit from the life histories of these two remarkable women.

El Tovar began its life as a Harvey House when it opened in 1905 in conjunction with the arrival of the Atchison, Topeka and Santa Fe Railway to the south rim of the Grand Canyon. El Tovar was an instant success and has been a major tourist draw for well over a century. It has 78 rooms many with a breath taking view of the Grand Canyon. The hotel was designated a National Historic Place in 1974. In 1983 it was featured in a scene for the comedic movie *National Lampoon's Vacation*. And while on this day it was merely the rallying point for our tour group, on my next visit

to the Grand Canyon it will be my residence at least for one night.

Also I want to take the train from Williams, Arizona. A train

departs Williams, Arizona every morning for a two and a quarter

hour ride up to the Grand Canyon next to the El Tovar. I can only

imagine that the views are magnificent. The return to Williams is

in the afternoon. The train service comes in a variety of options

from basic transportation to a luxury parlor car. I am convinced

this is how my family and I will make our next entry into the

wondrous world of the Grand Canyon on our next visit.

It took about an hour after our arrival before our entire group had

reassembled at the El Tovar. We had plenty of time to enjoy a

good meal at the El Tovar but we had no idea how long it would be

before our group was reassembled and we were told to expect a

lunch as a part of the total tour package. Thus informed we

skipped the dining opportunity. That turned out to be a huge mistake.

Our guide seemed to drive forever to our next observation site. Time, of course, expands exponentially when one is hungry and getting hungrier. Consequently even the spectacle and majesty of the Grand Canyon was becoming less compelling. Along the way we did stop at yet another Mary Colter creation, the 70 foot tall Desert View Watchtower. A climb to the top of this tower is rewarded with a spectacular 360 degree panoramic view. But we were hungry and sadly that was rapidly becoming our only concern.

Finally we were fed sometime after 3 PM. Big deal, that's not so late. Oh yes it is given our practice of rising early and eating very light. Kari and I were up by 6 AM that day and our last meal in

Kingman, Arizona was little more than a donut. It was now nine

hours later and we had been doing a lot of walking. We were

raging with hunger but to her credit Kari did not complain.

Frankly I am not so sure how much longer I would have gone

without getting openly cantankerous. Relief at last, but it was a

pretty light meal after all. I mention this only because it is one

more reason why I almost always avoid "packaged" tours. Our

discomfort detracted from one of nature's grandest attractions.

That condition would simply not have happened were we on our

own. Circumstances interfered with that option on this visit. So be

it.

Finally we were deposited back at the Red Feather Lodge and we

immediately walked to a nearby steak house where be both ordered

and then ravenously consumed a great big steak. Ah now that is

much better. It was even kind of fun to eaves drop on two

gentlemen who came in and sat down at a table next us. They

were talking about the experience one of them had that day flying a P-51 Mustang. Naturally flying talk is always fun for me but even Kari was smiling. She was almost fully there now as one of us weird people who would rather be flying than doing just about anything else.

Back at the hotel Kari got in her now daily swim while I went over the somewhat more challenging flight plan for tomorrow. Despite a somewhat annoying fixation on the next days flight both Kai and I had no trouble getting to sleep after a very full day of walking, hiking touring and just plain thoroughly enjoying the truly Grand Canyon. Tomorrow it was off to the reservation. There is plenty of Indian presence everywhere in America's southwest, but tomorrow we were landing right in the heart of Navajoland. Kari and I were both looking forward to a total unknown and yet excitement at yet another new adventure together so for now, good night.

Day Four

GCN – OV7

(Grand Canyon Airport, AZ –to- Kayenta Airport, AZ)

Our departure from the Grand Canyon National Park Airport was more complex than any other departure on this trip. First there was something weird going on in my head ever since day one. Each night before falling asleep I was increasingly obsessing about the next day's flight. My concerns went to the condition of the airplane and possible in-flight conditions. Worry would be a fair statement and there was absolutely positively no cause for any worry. Yet there it was. I could only attribute it to the presence of my eleven year old child. No she didn't do anything, but the simple fact that her life was literally in my hands coupled with the unforgiving terrain below us brought upon me a growing if mainly irrational worry. Still it was weird. I have being flying for more than 42 years and never ever

did I worry about a flight, even previous flights with Kari and
Kimberly and Nenita onboard. I had to hold this worry within
because I was certain that sharing it with Kari would have
generated a much greater concern in her mind. That only
exacerbated the situation

But speaking of exacerbation, my wife did not help with her daily
projection of a deep fear of flight. Kari had gotten into the habit of
calling mom just prior to each take off and then again immediately
upon landing. When she made the call after landing mom would
hoot and holler and cheer enthusiastically like the crowd in Paris
when Charles Lindbergh landed. I am sure that at least to some
degree mom's fear crept into the mix. The last time mom flew
with us was maybe six months previous when we flew up to Santa
Maria, California for a great brunch at the airport Radisson Hotel
and a very pleasant drive through the nearby wine country. The
trip home was exceptionally beautiful with a spectacular sun

setting over the Pacific Ocean to our right and a brilliant full moon

rising over the mountains to our left. Even the typically nervous

flyer Nenita found joy in these awesome sights. Yet after we

landed and were heading home in our automobile I asked her

where she wanted to go next. Her response was "No, no thanks, I

don't want to fly." It usually takes about six months between trips.

She likes them all and then defaults back to her deep fear of flying

in between. Now when her daughter and her husband were out in

the Wild West flying around she was having daily panic attacks

and sharing them with us. That was the second significant element

making this departure even more complex than most.

The only more or less rational reason contributing to the

complexity of this departure was the structure of the airspace we

were flying in and around. Thus far our routing had been

essentially a simple point to point or very close to a straight line

point to point routing. That would not be possible here. Our next stop, Kayenta, Arizona was directly to our north east or more precisely a heading of 049 degrees. Unfortunately taking that heading would put us directly into the protected airspace above the Grand Canyon. Doing that would have deeply irritated the National Park Service, the FAA, a whole bunch of Indians and probably several spirits as well. It was not an option. We needed to remain south of that restricted airspace but in taking a heading south of but parallel to the Grand Canyon restricted airspace we needed to take care not to inadvertently fly into the Military Operations Area nearby to the right of our flight path. Oddly flying into a Military Operations Area is legal but in my view it is real stupid. I mean seriously now in a dispute between a Cessna Cardinal and an F-16 who is going to win? Yeah! The F-16 wins every time. Sure steering the proper course was not an overwhelming task but it definitely did add to the complexity of our departure.

Oh and I really should not forget that we were departing from an airport already more than 6600 feet up in the sky and directly in front of us on our flight path was a rising mound of rock covered with nice tall Ponderosa pine trees. Those factors also contribute to the interest level on departure.

But as it turned out getting to the airport was the most difficult task of our departure that day. As usual Kari and I got up very early, about 5:45 AM or so. We quickly showered and packed and we were in the lobby area by about 6:20 AM. The very first thing I did was to ask the front desk staff at the Red Feather Lodge if they could help us get to the airport. At first the young man at the desk said in mild shock, "Why that is almost a four and a half hour drive," "Excuse me" I said, "but the airport is only a mile away." "Oh" he replied, "I thought you meant Phoenix." I'm guessing this guy was very new to the area. Now you would think that with the airport so close someone, the Duty Manager maybe, or a bellman, or maybe even the clerk might have offered a ride, but nope that wasn't going to happen. I have never heard of anything above a flop house this close to an airport not offering shuttle service, but such is the policy not only of the Red Feather Inn but all of the area hotels I was told. Now walking a mile or two is no big deal for either Kari or me, but our bags were pretty heavy and the thought of carrying them that distance was just plain unacceptable. The only option the hotel staff offered was to give us the telephone number for a taxi service located nearby some 20 miles away. We really had no choice so we called.

The taxi driver was actually embarrassed to request the full fare he was supposed to charge, a minimum of twenty dollars for a one mile ride. With clear reluctance he asked us for ten dollars which I paid and we left for the airplane. The Red Feather Lodge, despite the awesome work of Nancy Halstead the day before, really needs to revisit the concept of service. Apparently that would apply to all the hotels in the area as well. But once again the old adage was reconfirmed; the hardest part of most flights is getting to the airport.

Because of my previously mentioned angst my pre flight was even more thorough than usual. I checked magnetos twice each. Every flight and engine instrument and gauge was reviewed thoroughly. The flight controls were checked and rechecked outside and inside the airplane. I found the oil down one quart. The airplane was perfectly safe with the oil down one quart but today I had gone back to the FBO bought a quart of oil and added it. Fuel quantity and quality was checked and then checked again. My God I was becoming obsessive.

Finally I called ground control and we were cleared to runway two one. I found myself actually assessing how the airplane rolled on its way to the runway. Yup, the wheels were still round and the brakes worked well. Well we could either taxi back, shut it down, take a $2000 cab ride to Phoenix and fly home commercially, or get on with it. Come on Ron snap out of this. "Grand Canyon tower, Cardinal one three hotel kilo ready at two one" I spoke into my microphone. "Cardinal one three hotel kilo cleared for take off runway two one, left turn approved" came the immediate reply from the tower and we were on our way to Kayenta, Arizona, Navajo Nation. Complex departure and angst or not here we go.

KAYENTA, ARIZONA, NAVAJO NATION
CESSNA CARDINAL N13HK

Yeah okay I will admit that I wish we were able to climb a little

faster. Those gosh darn Ponderosa pine trees, while very pretty,

would make for a miserable landing area. Still we were able to

clear them with ample margin. But you sure can tell the

performance difference when departing from an airport 6609 MSL, even on a relatively cool morning. Trying it during the afternoon heat and winds could prove and has proven deadly.

For the first time on this adventure we got about ten minutes of fairly steady turbulence on out departure. To both my surprise and joy Kari took it with ease and grace, never showing even the slightest glimmer of fear or panic. In fact she remained wide eyed through out as we got one last spectacular view of the Grand Canyon on our way towards the Painted Desert and then Kayenta. She in fact mocked the temporary roughness by singing a little ditty something like; "Bump bump, bumpity bump – weeeeeeeeeee!"

What a great spirit.

The bumpity bumps happily were only with us maybe ten minutes before we returned to totally smooth calm relaxing flight. Both the

Grand Canyon restricted airspace and the Military Operations Area were rapidly passing and would soon become a mere memory for us on this trip. Ahead was the tiny Navajo city of Tuba City, important to us only because there was one of the navigation aids, a VOR located at Tuba City and because it offered us some visual confirmation that we were indeed flying on course.

Tuba City, Arizona, Navajo Nation is located within the Painted Desert and is called To' Naneesdizi by the native people who represent the overwhelming majority of its inhabitants. I am told and believe that the translation of To' Naneesdizi from Navajo to English is tangled waters. This is, so the story goes, because of many springs that lie just below the surface of this area. While not officially by U. S. standards a true city it is a city according to the local Navajo people and it is after all their land so it really is a City, period, end of story. Tuba City sits at about 4900 feet above sea level and covers a small 8.9 square miles with a population of only about 2000 people. From more than one mile above it Tuba City seemed very small, yet there it was guiding us on. Then again to the people on the ground in Tuba City we may well have been invisible. It truly is all relative.

Over Tuba City we were about 60 straight line flight miles from Kayenta or roughly 32 more flying minutes. In a car on the ground both the distance and the time would swell dramatically. Just one more reason to love air travel. Clearly in front of us was yet another rise in the terrain, a rise we would over fly and just beyond which I was sure was the town of Kayenta with its airport. "We are almost there Kari" I said. She just smiled.

I did a couple of things in preparation of our visit to Kayenta. One was to call our hotel and ask if they provided transportation from the airport to the hotel which they confirmed they did so long as I called once I was on the ground. There other was to check for

specific information about the airport such as facilities and

possible instrument approaches. There were none. There was

however an admonishment to over fly the field before landing to

assure that stray animals such as cows, coyotes and perhaps sheep

were not present. The warning went on to say to beware of

possible non-flying vehicles on the runway. Boy TSA would freak

out at this place. So over the ridge and down the slope we flew

meeting one or two more small bumps along the way just to let us

know we had arrived.

The airport elevation was 5710 feet MSL and the normal pattern

altitude for us was 6700 feet per the altimeter. I dropped a wee bit

lower to get a good look at the runway and also trying to find a

windsock. I never found a windsock and if there was one at

Kayenta I could not tell you where. Absent any wind information I

just figured that since in the area winds normally came from the west I would set up to land on runway 23. I also made radio announcements almost certainly to no one on the CTAF frequency of 122.9 MHz just in case there was any other traffic. It sure didn't look like there was any other traffic, but given my luck had I not made calls this would have been the day some huge flying club out of, oh I don't know, Prescott, Arizona maybe, would have chosen for a massive fly in to Kayenta. So I made calls while scanning the 7140 foot runway. It looked narrow even though it was the same width as the runway of my home field, 75 feet. Part of the reason for that appearance I am sure was that weeds were creeping in from the edges taking over a fair portion of the runway. To some extent this would be a soft field landing on an asphalt runway. But I saw no cows, no coyotes, no sheep, no people and no vehicles. I also saw only one other airplane, a twin engine Beechcraft King Air 200 parked off of the west end of the field. There was no control tower, no line shack, not even a porta-potty. This was going to be fun.

We turned base leg and then quickly to our final approach. Darn that runway looks narrow but long I thought. I also noted that roughly a third of the surface was weeds poking through asphalt. Except for the runway there was no other way to taxi, no taxiway in other words. This was truly a very basic airport. This was really going to be fun.

We touched down gently and precisely where we needed to be leaving a good deal of runway ahead. We slowed with no need to apply any braking and rolled steadily toward the small tie down area ahead and to our left. Traffic was not a problem, there wasn't any. We had arrived in Kayenta, Arizona, Navajo Nation where the local time was one hour later than it was where we had departed. But far more than a mere one hour time zone change we had in some way truly traveled back in time as the rest of day would demonstrate.

As I have said I tend to travel guided mainly by serendipity. Consequently while I knew that Kayenta was within the Navajo Nation variously also known as Navajoland and the Navajo Reservation, I did not know until I arrived there that Kayenta was also the gateway to Monument Valley. In fact some of the "monuments" in Monument Valley are plainly visible from the town of Kayenta. Nor did we know until arrival that we would lose an hour due to a time zone change or that Kayenta was a town of some 5000 people most obviously of American Indian heritage. In fact Kayenta is the only incorporated township in the Navajo Nation. It is a dry area meaning no alcohol can be legally sold within its boundaries. It is also a dry area meaning the annual average rain fall is quite minimal. And despite its humble character it is to my brief experience one of the friendliest places in the American south west. In the native Navajo language what we call Kayenta is called To' Dine'eshzhee. And then there is the big picture, the Navajo nation in its entirety.

By their own words which I can not and do not dispute the Navajo are the largest and most influential Indian tribe in North America. By the way, attention please political correctness police. Please note that the Navajo people themselves on their website (www.americanwest.com/pages/navajo2.htm) call themselves an Indian tribe and not a group of Native Americans. Indeed throughout our travels in the southwest I politely asked many Indians if they preferred being referred to as "Native Americans" and to a person they said "No." If they had any preference it was for their tribal affiliation such as Navajo or Hopi or Ute or Apache. Sadly the Navajo Indians were nearly eliminated in the 1860's with their numbers reduced to around 8000. Today they are closer to a quarter of a million strong and youthful with more than 60% of their population under the age of 24 years.

The land of the Navajo is today a rather substantial 26,000 square miles spread over the states of Arizona, New Mexico and Utah. The official "capital" of the Navajo Nation is in Window Rock, Arizona where the 88 member council meets at least four times each year.

Common to all American Indians the Navajo hold Mother Earth in the highest regard. The medicine men are still a significant part of Navajo life although today they often share the stage if you will with more modern western medicine. Medicine men are believed to be uniquely qualified and imbued with supernatural powers which really make them not all that different from the neighborhood physician for most people.

The Navajo language supports the broad application of humor. The Navajo so respect the power of humor that when a Navajo child laughs for the very first time it is deemed a time for honor and celebration. I am in complete agreement with this element of the Navajo culture and hope that it spreads widely. We as a people desperately need more humor. Just imagine how much better off our world would be if we could just get some of those deadly wild eyed fanatics to laugh a little.

A point of great pride amongst the Navajo is the great heroic contributions they made in the United States Marine Corps during world war two when they stymied the enemy as code talkers. Often operating on the front lines these brave and patriotic Navajo Indians would communicate using their native language thereby utterly confounding any Japanese who may have been listening to the transmission.

Their story was dramatically told in the 2002 movie *Windtalkers* starring Nicholas Cage. A less dramatic but more authentic telling of their heroic tale can be found at the Code Talkers museum found next to the Burger King restaurant in Kayenta. I was familiar with their story yet both Kari and I found the modest presentation very compelling.

We had landed right smack dab in the middle of this proud and culturally rich Navajo Nation the moment our wheels touched the runway at the Kayenta Airport. Next we were to discover an element of Navajo culture not discussed in the history books or the travel guides, their true friendliness. Before buttoning up Cardinal N13HK I placed a call to the Best Western hotel where we had booked a room. After explaining where we were and what we needed I was told someone would be there shortly. We weren't

even completely done with the tie down task when a lady arrived

in a Jeep and introduced herself as Desire` LaFont of the Best

Western Wetherill Inn. We loaded our bags in the back and

climbed in her Jeep and soon we were standing at the reception

desk of the hotel.   At the suggestion of Desire" we had left our

bags in the Jeep primarily because it was still early and there was a

chance our room was not yet clean and ready. Kari reminded me

that she had left her brush at the hotel in Kingman and she sure

could use a brush. I asked for and got directions to a small

convenience store very close to the hotel.

There were two doors. Over the door on our right there was a sign

proclaiming "Market." But over the door on our left the sign read:

"Radio Shack." We went in the door on our right and quickly

found a decent brush for Kari and immediately thereafter a

somewhat different looking but nonetheless effective Slurpy

machine. Hair care and thirst quenching all in one fast stop, now that's the ticket. We paid for our merchandise and left through the same door we had entered through. I then abruptly moved to my right and entered through the door labeled "Radio Shack." Kari was quick to point out that it took us back to the very same store, just a different section. "Yeah" I said "I know, but now I need batteries" leaving Kari shaking her head in utter disbelief. Sometimes dads have that effect on their kids and it is only fair that it should work both ways.

Hair about to be brushed, thirst quenched and batteries replenished we walked back to the hotel where Desire' asked us if we would like to take a tour of Monument Valley or simply take her Jeep and drive ourselves around Monument Valley. As I have said I really loath tours, so this was a no brainer. But I was pleasantly shocked at the offer of her Jeep. Heck it was this very morning we could not get a one mile ride from the hotel in Grand Canyon. Now here was Desire' LaFont, Operations Manager of the Best Western in

Kayenta just handing me the keys to her Jeep. I'm thinking she

needs to hold seminars in Grand Canyon. Then she tells us to just

turn left when leaving the motel parking lot and follow Route 163

18 miles and we will be in the core of Monument Valley. She

further explained that there was tourist information and a lodge on

our left and a Navajo park on our right when we get to the "T"

intersection at the 18 mile mark. The Navajo park charges an entry

fee she advises. It all sounded simple and reasonable to me so with

absolutely positively no real idea of what we were getting

ourselves into we jumped into Desire's Jeep and we were on our

way.

It turned out that Route 163 was a well maintained two lane

highway that took us basically straight north out of Kayenta and

eventually into the State of Utah all without ever even coming

close to leaving the Navajo Nation or just Kayenta Township for that matter. Kari was amazed and delighted that we had made it to Utah. That was actually a bit of an unexpected surprise for both of us. There goes that serendipity again.

Although the road was mostly straight and flat there wasn't a dull moment during the entire drive. The scenery was other worldly and captivating from the moment we pulled out of the driveway of the Best Western and it only got better with each mile. Driving into Monument Valley from Kayenta was kind of like peeling an onion only the beauty of it increased ten fold with each new layer. Maybe we should have employed an Indian guide but we were rather put off by guides that day. Perhaps we should have driven further than the "T" intersection but that too we passed on. Yet neither Kari nor I was in any way disappointed. The colors and forms made the experience feel like driving directly into a spectacular painting of the old west. Hues of red and amber dominated the many monuments, the ground is green and red and

brown and gray and the sky was azure blue with only the right
amount of brilliant white accent from a passing cloud.   Neither
Monet nor Renoir could have equaled this massive living canvas.
Soon Kari and I agreed that in its own special way Monument
Valley surpassed even the awesome beauty of the Grand Canyon.
I think part of that had to do with the relative absence of the
teaming masses of the Grand Canyon at peak season along with the
thus far much friendlier experiences with the nice people we had
met. Still and all objectively as possible Monument Valley at the
absolute least equals the glory of the Grand Canyon and that is
saying quite a lot. We had come thoroughly unprepared and we
were satiated with sensory delight. We will be back but our visit
was far from over.

To better understand the powerful visual impact of Monument
Valley please consider this:

Stagecoach

The Searchers

2001: A Space Odyssey

Easy Rider

One Upon a Time in the West

The Eiger Sanction

Revolver

Back to the Future III

National Lampoon's Vacation

Forrest Gump

Thelma & Louise

Mission Impossible II

All had scenes set in Monument Valley. But Hollywood had not discovered Monument Valley by serendipity like Kari and I had, oh no. It took the vision and drive and determination of Harry Goulding and his wife Mike to bring not just Hollywood but director John Ford and super star John Wayne to Monument Valley. The year was 1937 and the Great Depression was winding down when he and his wife Mike made the trip from Monument Valley to Hollywood using their bedrolls, truck and their last $60 to make the trip and their share of guts to get through the maze and touch the big time director.

Indeed they were actually being escorted out of the office so the story goes when the location manager caught a glimpse of the photographs Harry had with him of Monument Valley. The photographs totally mesmerized the location manager and just ten days later a crew together with John Wayne was in Monument Valley to begin production on the Academy Award winning *Stagecoach.* Now that may not be serendipity but it is certainly a great big slice of good luck. It was also very good fortune for local Navajo who had suffered more than most through the Great Depression. John Ford paid them SAG Union wages for their work on the film. This explains one of the unique aspects of the Goulding Lodge complex as it exists today.

We turned to our left at the "T" intersection and a drove up to the Goulding Lodge complex and parked Desire's Jeep pretty much right in front of the small museum. We entered the museum and made a donation and then began our tour. There were two or three rooms containing the original furnishings from when Harry and Mike Goulding lived there. Mike's actual name was Leone but it seems that Harry had a hard time spelling Leone so he just named her Mike and the name stuck. The old west décor was fascinating but the dominant theme was John Wayne and John Wayne and John Ford movies. In fact the place is virtually a shrine to John Wayne which I found intriguing given that John Wayne had made more than one movie in which he portrayed a man shooting at

Indians with lethal intent. But the Navajo are real people who obviously can easily separate movie fantasy from the reality in which they had received desperately needed economic boost from that industry. The museum is small but like everything else about Monument Valley it contains a large dose of wonder.

It was now time for lunch so off we went to the *Stagecoach* dining room. We were given great seating with a magnificent view of the Valley through floor to ceiling windows. Soon after we had been seated a group of about ten Japanese tourists came in and sat down for lunch. Clearly Monument Valley is a true international tourist destination and yet Kari and I, two Americans who lived much closer than the Japanese group were seeing this amazing place for the very first time.

I honestly can't remember what Kari ordered but I was intrigued by and so ordered a Navajo Taco. I had no idea what that was but you can't call something an adventure if you aren't willing to stretch a bit. The service was superb and didn't take long for my chosen dish to be presented. It was almost as impressive as the local geography. HOLY COW! It was humongous. The foundation is a piece of Navajo Fry bread a little bigger in diameter than a typical dinner plate, somewhere between ten to twelve inches in diameter. That will get your attention but then on top of that they pile about a pound of hamburger a similar amount of beans, onions, tomatoes, avocado, cheese and lettuce all which peaks out about eight to ten inches off of the plate. One Navajo Taco could easily fill up a hungry family of four. There was no way I was going to eat all that. What I did eat was delicious but it was just overwhelming. My reaction brought a huge grin to Kari's face as she chided me to clean my plate. Yeah, right!

As we sat with me picking at the mountain in front of me I saw a small airport outside to my right front. I didn't specifically check it but I would guess that the field elevation was somewhere near or maybe a little above 5000 feet MSL. Also it had gotten much warmer since our arrival in the area. I would guess from this that density altitude, that is the altitude the airplane "thinks" it is at for performance purposes was probably somewhere between eight and nine thousand feet. That is darn high for a small, single normally aspirated engine like the one stuck on the front of the green and white Cessna 172 I saw just starting its take off roll on what to me seemed just a little too short of a runway. I watched with rapidly increasing interest as he rolled down the runway. At the halfway point he was still firmly on the ground. My interest grew and I abruptly said to Kari, "Watch this guy takeoff, I hope he makes it." Together we saw him continue his take off roll until not much more than maybe 30 feet before the end of the runway and an apparent fence. He cleared it all, barely. Whew! Now that is something I would not do. My guess was he was a local pilot who had done this many times and was confident in the outcome. But for me, just paint a great big yellow stripe right down the middle of my back.

After lunch, with only about a third of the Navajo Taco consumed by a joint effort between Kari and me, we strolled around the grounds of the Goulding Lodge including a short visit to the Trading Post. Down the end of the parking lot we took some pictures and then walked back to Desire's Jeep and drove back down the road towards Highway 163 and the Navajo park on the other side. We crossed Route 163 and drove up to the gate to the park but chose not to enter this day. It was time to head back to our hotel in Kayenta.

MOVIE STAR SUPREME, THE LATE GREAT JOHN WAYNE

WITH MOVIE STAR IN THE MAKING, KARI IRWIN

Have you ever noticed how when you drive back down the same road you drove up to get somewhere the scenery is entirely different? That perceptual reality kept us fully entertained on our not very long drive back to the Best Western Wetherill Inn. Kari and I discussed just how nice it was for Desire` to loan us her Jeep for the day. We decided we should thank her in two ways. One was to fill the gas tank which we did. Then we also stopped at a local food market, a fairly large one like you might find in any American city and went to the bakery department. There Kari and I picked out a half dozen great big delicious looking cookies for Desire'.

Back at the hotel we got our room keys, plastic cards actually these days, and removed our bags from the Jeep and took them to our room. We freshened up a bit, knocking some of the road dust off of ourselves and then went back to the hotel lobby which also served as a small Trading Post/Gift Shop. Being in no particular hurry Kari and I looked at lots of nice things, especially the very pretty Indian jewelry. First Kari found a couple of really pretty turquoise beaded "pony tails" which we bought. The shopping continued. We knew that we had to buy something for mom but what? We could not just ignore her but then again we didn't want to reward her for not joining us on this trip. Finally we settled on a very nice wooden dream box. It was pretty, it was small, it was inexpensive and it was perfect. She could start dreaming for a bigger airplane that she wouldn't be afraid to fly in. Unfortunately in mom's mind that means a Boeing 747 which could only make a really ugly landing at the Kayenta airport. Oh well, the shopping continued. I saw a couple of rings that appealed to me and while I was checking them out Kari had found a couple of necklaces for herself. We compromised, we bought it all. She had a couple of modest but nice necklaces and I had a very nice silver ring inscribed with a bear claw design.

The ladies helping us were like everyone else we met in Kayenta, very pleasant and fun to deal with. The one thing that kept ringing through both of our heads was "this place is real." Sure it is small and there isn't a whole lot right in the town, but it is all genuine, certainly more so than in our more or less home town of Hollywood. Did we want to move there? No. But we were both very glad for the opportunity to visit there just once in our lives and we both decided that someday we would come back with mom and sister. That, of course, will mean driving probably from Phoenix, Arizona after a commercial flight but a man has to do what a man has to do. So I guess I will have to pay for someone else to fly us around.

It was getting late and the sun was heading for the places from whence we had come. Even the gigantic Navajo Taco had begun to lose its rejuvenative powers so we headed out to a small restaurant basically next to the hotel. In keeping with all things

Kayenta it was a modest place without pretense but the food was good and reasonably priced.

That requirement taken care of, it was time for Kari's nightly swim. The other habit that had grown stronger each day of the trip was after the swim she would watch Disney Channel for an hour or so as we wound down for our evenings sleep. With the TV finally silenced and Kari now fully at rest I peeked out our hotel room window up into the black sky above, a sky alive with a huge blanket of twinkling stars the vast majority of which will never be seen by us city dwellers. It is no wonder that the American Indian tends to be very spiritual I thought. Then it was time for me to sleep and dream, perhaps, of all the miracles we had been blessed to see this extraordinary day.

Day Five

OV7 – DRO

(Kayenta Airport, AZ –to- Durango, CO)

D reams have never been a subject of interpretation for me. To my way of thinking all dreams are is a hodge podge of random thoughts thrown together in often a fascinating mix and projected within an otherwise resting mind. Still dreams do have impact; just ask any child snapped into consciousness by a horrific nightmare. Even adults can have more than a little scare injected into them by a particularly disturbing dream. For many years one recurring theme I have actually enjoyed even though it has its scary elements is a series of dreams about airplanes flying absurdly low. Let me explain.

Airplanes as I am sure most people instinctively understand are supposed to go up when they take off. Indeed airplanes are supposed ascend rather briskly. Neither airplanes nor our normal flight practices accept continued near ground level flight after takeoff. Airplanes are simply supposed to be in the air that is where they work best. In fact a good friend of mine, flight instructor extraordinaire Mario Martinez was in an airplane one day that did not want to climb up as it should. Indeed it quickly became evident to him that this particular airplane on this particular day wanted very much to go back to earth. The problem was that it had only recently left the airport and runway behind. Armed with that horrifying knowledge Mario did the only thing he could, he found the best possible alternate place to land, for land he surely would, and he landed. The landing was excellent, right up to the point when the nose wheel of the airplane struck a rock and the airplane flipped upside down. In the end the airplane was destroyed but both Mario and the airplane owner and student Nato Flores escaped essentially unharmed. They were very lucky and fortunate that Mario Martinez is a skilled pilot. It was eventually determined that the cause of this frightening and life threatening accident was some very sloppy work performed by a not very capable mechanic. All is well that ends well the saying goes, but that accident underscores the reality that airplanes really are supposed to go up.

So for many years now I have had dreams about airplanes that did not go up. They were always airliners, big jets as a matter of fact and the reason they didn't go up was because the pilots held them down low. There was never a mechanical problem in these dreams; they simply flew low because the pilots had been told to fly low; ridiculously low. For example in these dreams the airplanes would often fly under bridges and over passes and between buildings in a manner that was just flat out impossible in the real world. But that is the magic of dreams; the real world does not constrain them. Still the dreams were frightening. Visions of buildings and trees and telephone poles flashing by at two or three or four hundred miles an hour are scary. In one slightly modified version of this series of dreams I on a few occasions dreamt of a

Cathay Pacific Boeing 747 leaving Los Angeles bound for Hong Kong only to end up in a large park just outside New York City. Now that dream is so bizarre and funny it actually snapped me into consciousness and laughter the first time I dreamt it.

However, whether amusing or scary or some combination thereof dreams can and do impact the conscious mind and the dream I had this morning just before awakening was absolutely impacting my conscious mind. No dream in my many years had ever involved a violent airplane crash. True the flying styles were bizarre and frightening but there was never a violent crash. Even in the dream where the 747 lands in a park it does so smoothly and gently contrary, of course, to real world physics. But for the first time this very morning my dream involved a crashing airplane. It was not and I emphasize NOT a small general aviation airplane and certainly not a Cessna Cardinal. It was in fact a blazing airliner falling out of the sky. Still it was for the very first time a dream of a violent crash. I have no doubt but that this was caused primarily by the growing angst I had over the absolute safety of my daughter Kari, exacerbated every day by mom's abject terror. None of this was rational but rational or not, it was with me this morning as we prepared for out flight to Durango, CO.

We got up early as usual. Kari always showered at night after her swim so it was my turn to shower each morning which I did as Kari got dressed and packed her bag. After my shower I got dressed and packed the rest of our stuff and we headed down for our typical Continental breakfast and to check out of the hotel.

The weather was as it had been throughout this entire trip so far, absolutely perfect. There was no significant wind and no clouds of any kind anywhere. Today's flight would be only slightly longer than yesterdays. Today we would fly about 122 NM in about one hour and ten minutes. There were no tricky airspace maneuvers to follow and the airplane itself had been running flawlessly with no reason to believe that condition would change. My mechanic Glenn Roberts back it at Whiteman Airport had done a splendid job keeping our airplane in excellent operating condition. There was no reason to even think anything would fail today. There was however my dream this morning, and mom's usual daily dose of runaway fear. And just before departure there was just one more little thing.

Food consumed and final details at the hotel taken care of and Desire' LaFont cheerfully returned us to the airport and our beautiful Cardinal N13HK. She hung around standing outside her Jeep as Kari and I went about our routine process of loading and securing our bags and performing a pre flight inspection of the airplane. The airplane seemed to be in excellent, completely airworthy condition. About the only thing I noticed was that this morning there were now two King Air 200 aircraft there rather the one that had been there yesterday. Today there were two air ambulances standing by. Great!

We got everything outside the airplane ready and Kari climbed in and took her position in the co pilot's seat to my right. Before I boarded the airplane I asked Desire's why she was still there. She said: "Oh my dad is a pilot you know and sometimes these things don't work right, so I will just hang here until you are out of sight." Now that was a very kind thing to do but it in a weird way just piled on my already over active brain. I had been steadily building angst. Then there was the first ever airplane crash dream this morning followed by mom's daily dose of fear. Then we are greeted by not just one but two air ambulance planes and finally I am being told that airplanes don't always work right so Desire' will stick around awhile longer. Okay that's it I am getting out of here right now before I change my mind.

You can bet we did a very thoroughly almost absurdly thorough

inside pre flight. It was a very long taxi out to the end of the

runway during which I checked and rechecked the flight controls,

the gauges, the gyros, the flaps, the brakes, the doors, the radios,

our charts, the flight plan, Kari's seat belt, the cowl flaps, my door,

her door, the trim controls, the vacuum meter, the electrical

system, the fuel tank gauges, the oil temperature, the oil pressure,

the exhaust gas temperature, the cylinder head temperature, the

printed check list, the Pilot's Operating Handbook and everything

else I could think of and then I did it all again in the run up area

before taxing back in the opposite direction on the runway.   Yeah

I was being a little freaky but I hope I was keeping it from Kari. I

think I was being successful because she was a picture of serenity.

Darn she is something else.

I was lined up with center line running the length of the runway

right in the middle of the weeds and asphalt. I applied full power

and released the brakes and we were off. We actually got off the

ground fairly quickly and we did in fact climb without hesitation.

Good! No actually, GREAT! As we flew abeam Desire' I thanked

her the only way I could right then and there, I wagged my wings

at her. There went Kari's serenity. "Dad!" she almost screamed

both a question and a statement. "I was just waving good bye to

Desire" I explained and that instantly mollified Kari. Desire'

waved and by the time we had turned down wind towards our next

destination of Durango, Colorado she was gone. Kari and I will

forever remember our short but wonderful stay in the tiny but

warm town of Kayenta, Arizona, Navajo Nation USA. But for

now this was a new day and we were now flying directly towards

yet another charming town, Durango, Colorado and its still to be

discovered by us treats and pleasures. Funny but predictable I

guess, but the instant our wheels left the ground my fears and

anxieties vanished along with the bonds of gravity. We were on our way to the furthest point in our trip. By the time we landed at Durango we will have flown about 600 nautical miles from our starting point and we will have done it in just under six hours of flight time. This was our apex, our turning point. After Durango we would begin working our way back home. But for now it was Durango, Colorado here we come.

We were now using the Denver Sectional Aeronautical Chart to back up our GPS and other navigational resources. Our flight path took us just a little north of the Carrizo Mountains and almost directly over the "Four Corners." The Four Corners is the one and only place on this earth where a person can stand on one foot and be in four states of these United States at the exact same time. At this precise place the borders of Utah, Arizona, New Mexico and Colorado meet. There is even a monument to commemorate that auspicious fact. This too has made it to our "someday" list of places to go and things to see. We were making excellent time today, with a ground speed approaching 140 knots. Clearly we had favorable tail winds and that pleased both Kari and me.

The ground beneath us began to change dramatically, going from mainly brown to increasing levels of green. Soon we were actually over Mesa Verde, or the green mesa and it was indeed much greener than what it had been since just before Palmdale, California. We were speeding our way directly at the Rocky Mountains and yet the air remained calm and even the mountains looming off in the distance, some with tops around 14,000 feet were much more attractive than intimidating.

Now off to our right was the City of Farmington, New Mexico and we were rapidly approaching our destination of Durango, Colorado and the Durango La Plata County Airport. I tuned in the Durango ASOS (weather and airport information) on 120.625 MHz and was at once pleased and somewhat surprised to learn that there was basically no wind at the Durango Airport. "This is a good thing" I thought. Next I tuned in the Durango Unicom on 122.8 MHz and heard absolutely no chatter whatsoever for the Durango La Plata County Airport. Kari and I were both somewhat amused by the ongoing radio calls from some guy in a Bonanza apparently flying the traffic pattern at some other airport we couldn't find on our chart. Well heck we had essentially a two mile high antenna affixed to our airplane so receiving radio traffic from many miles away is not all that unusual. Still it became a source of mild entertainment for us as we continued to motor on for Durango.

The Durango La Plata County Airport is actually a fairly busy airport with commercial airline service from Delta, U. S. Air and United Express. It also draws a lot of high end charter traffic and a robust amount of us little guys as well. Still it is a non towered field and to my surprise it also has an ILS approach.

The Instrument Landing System or simply ILS is a navigational aid that provides pilots with both vertical and lateral guidance by means of radio emissions broadcast over a very sophisticated antenna system at the airports where such systems are installed. They have been around for several decades and while they are currently being supplemented by GPS approaches and may well some day be replaced by newer technologies they currently serve many airports worldwide including the vast majority of airports with commercial airline traffic. It is a precision approach and it is an extremely useful tool permitting airplanes to land even when the visibility is very restricted due mainly to very poor weather. Odds are if you have ever been on a commercial airline flight you have ridden along on an ILS approach obviously without knowing it. To fly the approach the pilot refers to an instrument in the cockpit that has two needles. When the proper frequency is tuned into the right frequency and the station is confirmed these two needles show the aircrafts position relative to the optimum vertical and lateral paths to the selected airport and runway. In very simple terms all the pilot needs to do is to align those needles so that stay perfectly centered and look like a large "+" on the instrument. Keep those two needles centered and the pilot will eventually find the proper runway. Do please keep in mind that this is a very much over simplified explanation but it serves the purposes of this discussion. As I said this is a precision and relatively sophisticated approach and I therefore found it interesting that one existed at the Durango La Plata County Airport, Colorado. So I could not help myself, I had to fly this approach even though there wasn't cloud within 300 miles in any direction.

The mean airport elevation at the Durango La Plata County Airport is 6685 feet MSL. However the touch down zone elevation, that is the actual elevation at the point one is expected to touch down when flying the ILS Runway 2 approach is 6638 feet MSL or 47 lower than the mean airport elevation. Obviously the runway slopes up at some point. The Decision Altitude for the ILS Runway 2 approach at the Durango La Plata County Airport is 6838 feet MSL or a mere 200 feet above the touch down zone elevation. What that means is that if a pilot flies this approach in real instrument meteorological conditions with clouds and fog and rain or snow and he arrives at an altitude of 6838 hopefully with needles centered and he still can't see the runway environment he has to keep flying and follow the missed approach procedures. If you have ever been flying in an airliner and as it was coming in for a landing you noticed that the pilot added power back and went back up he was likely making a "missed approach."

Keeping in mind that the weather at Durango La Plata County Airport this day was perfect and the ILS approach was not required. Still being the hopefully good instrument pilot that I try hard to be I did brief myself on exactly what to do if I had to "go missed." It wasn't a comforting thought with really huge

mountains nearby. The procedure called for an immediate climb to

7500 feet followed by a climbing right turn to a heading of 140

degrees until reaching an altitude of 10,000 feet MSL intercepting

the 120 degree radial off of the Durango VOR and finally holding

at the SOVDE intersection a fictional spot in space known only to

some pilots and air traffic controllers. This is the "black magic"

part of instrument flight and one of the reasons I like flying in real

instrument conditions whenever possible.

The potentially deadly problem occurs when let's say the pilot

forgets the right turn. This would be a busy and stressful time in

the cockpit and things can be easily forgotten even things that

really shouldn't be forgotten. At Durango if the turn is forgotten

there is a near perfect chance of flying directly into very hard rock.

This kind of mistake does happen several times each year. But

today it could not happen to us because we could plainly see all of the terrain around us. That option does not exist when the clouds are thick and low, however. So I briefed myself on the missed approach procedure just for good form even though it certainly would not come into play this day. Oh and there is one other thing.

Since most ILS approaches are into airports with a control tower, the pilot would typically be in communication with that tower prior to and while landing. If it became necessary to make a missed approach the pilot would announce that to the tower and the tower would very likely give him a vector (a turn) before handing him off to another controller. Were there a tower at Durango for example, the tower controller would likely say something like: "Cardinal one three hotel kilo turn right heading one four zero, climb and maintain one zero thousand and contact Denver Center on one one eight point five seven five." Absent the tower it is entirely up to the pilot to know what to do, do it and contact Denver Center as needed. That's a lot of work in a fairly high stress environment and while flying around at or above a hundred miles an hour while being effectively blind. Cool stuff.

So on this brilliantly sunny and totally cloudless day I tuned in the ILS Localizer for the Durango La Plata County Airport on 109.1 MHz and adjusted my flight path to intercept localizer at the Outer Marker. All this stuff is on a specific type of chart known as an approach plate. I also needed to be at 8800 feet MSL by the time I reached the outer marker so I began a gentle descent. As all this was happening I explained it all to Kari pointing to the Localizer and Glide Slope indicator and telling her what to look for as we reached the right location and altitude. This was going to be very cool and fortunately for me I hit the mark right on the money. We got established on the localizer right at the Outer Marker and about ten feet high on the glide slope. The blue marker beacon light lit up and we heard the reassuring beep beep beep of the marker beacon in our headsets. I nailed the glide slope and the localizer and Kari had a big bright grin. Yeah sure we could see the airport but that's okay we were still flying the ILS approach.

"Durango traffic, Cardinal one three hotel kilo out of eight thousand eight hundred, outer marker on the ILS for runway two, Durango" I announced blindly to all who might care. We heard no reply, we saw no traffic we continued our approach. Sweet! As we approached the Decision Altitude the Middle Marker light and tone went off. This was really fun. The runway was right in front of us and there was obviously no need to "go missed" so I flattened out our angle of descent and bled off some airspeed before we rotated to a nose up attitude and gently placed our lovely Cardinal on Runway 02 of the Durango La Plata County Airport. Colorado! We had made it.

We took the first taxiway to our left and almost immediately there were two folks in a golf cart from the Durango Jet Center leading us to our tie down for the night. And as we taxied to our tie down Kari and I watched as a CRJ came to a halt basically abeam our position. He had just landed on runway 20 at the same airport. Same airport, same day, close to the same time but in the exact opposite direction; one of the other things that keeps life exciting at non towered airports I thought to myself.

As the ramp guy was driving us to the private terminal he was telling us about some of the more interesting aircraft that have visited the Durango La Plata County Airport. He was particularly impressed with a recent visit of a Boeing 757 "loaded with Swiss bankers" he said. I wondered how he knew them to be Swiss bankers. I mean I guess it kind of made sense. Surely they would spend tens of thousands of dollars to fly from one Alpine topography to another. But then it was a good story. I also learned

that we absolutely would need to rent a car. The airport at
Durango was 18 miles for the town of Durango and no, no hotel
offered a shuttle service. That all turned out to be a good thing as I
will explain shortly. Last but by no means least I also learned that
we had once again landed in Indian Country. The Durango La
Plata County Airport I was told was owned by and leased from the
Ute Indians. So we were back on the reservation. It sure was one
pretty reservation and there were a lot of very plush flying
machines in evidence.

Unlike the Navajo the Ute's were a loose association of nomadic
bands of Indians who roamed what today is known as Utah,
Colorado, Wyoming and New Mexico. Today the Southern Ute
Indians, those from the southern reservation located in south
western Colorado are the wealthiest of the tribes with assets of
approximately $8 billion dollars. The modern Ute tribe is a bona
fide group of business moguls and their assets include casino

operations, tourism, oil and gas and real estate ventures including the very airport we had just landed on. This information was at the very least interesting and could be important and yet I am certain it would not appear in Kari's sixth grade history book. Great value had once again been added to our adventure.

With all of the bureaucratic details, mainly fuel and payment, resolved our ramp man very kindly drove us to the nearby airline terminal so we could rent a car. The place was a hot bed of activity very much the opposite of what we had experienced flying in only about ten minutes earlier. There was a snack shop, a gift shop, long lines at the airline ticket counters and of course long lines at what is euphemistically called airport security as provided by TSA. Even Kari was amazed by what she saw as people lined up, shoes in hand, to pass through the TSA gauntlet, a process that does absolutely nothing to make commercial aviation any safer. "Daddy, we sure are lucky we don't have to do all that" she wisely observed. We indeed were lucky and I pray our luck holds because there are those out there pressing to impose this debilitating nonsense on the general aviation world. Should they prevail an adventure such as this could not happen, at least not for Kari and me. The financial and time costs would simply be too high and even if not the needless harassment would kill the spirit of the venture. "Yes Kari we are very lucky" I replied.

The task at hand was renting a car and that task proved far more difficult than I had originally envisioned. We approached the counters one at time. First Hertz told us they had no cars available, and then Avis and then Budget. Aw come on now, no cars how can that be? Our last hope was our last stop at National. They had a car but it needed to be serviced and would be available in twenty minutes. There being absolutely no other option I smiled and said: "Great we'll take it." We then handed the rental car person my driver's license and credit card and he completed the paperwork.

With nothing else to do until the car was ready Kari and I more fully explored the bustling terminal. We found it simply amazing. Just outside the sense was one of complete tranquility. Yet here within the walls of the terminal it was very much the same tempo as you would find at LAX or Chicago O'Hara or JFK airport. Sure smaller, a lot smaller, but the same basic energy was present. Step outside, serene, step back inside and it was frantic.

There was a gift shop nearby and I wanted a coffee mug. I have collected coffee mugs for years and I have many of them on my wall at home. My most exotic is from Cambodia but a mug from Durango, Colorado was equally as significant because it commemorated yet another destination visited. That is my one unshakeable rule I only collect mugs from places I have actually visited. I do not accept gifts of mugs from places I haven't been. I soon found and purchased a suitable memento and Kari and I headed back to the National car rental counter arriving at the same time our car arrived. We were given a map and brief instructions on how to get to Durango and as a suggested option to Silverton, Colorado and we were on are way.

THE DURANGO SILVERTON NARROW GAUGE RAILROAD

The day was still very young and while the sun was warm it was not nearly as hot as we had been living in for the last few days. And the scenery was pastoral and green and so the miles rolled by quickly and soon we were north bound on Route 550 at the south

end of the town of Durango, Colorado. As I said it was still early

and we knew that our hotel room would not be available until after

noon. Also the town of Silverton, Colorado was not all that far

beyond Durango. Now had there been a shuttle from the airport to

the hotel we almost certainly would not have made this decision

but being as we were in a rental car with nothing but road ahead

Kari and I decided to keep right on going and have our lunch in

Silverton.

First we had to transition through the minor but fascinating

metropolis of Durango. We had considered a ride on the fabled

narrow gauge Durango Silverton Railroad but we were not certain

of its schedule or the costs involved and we did have a car so we

figured we should use it and we did. Passing through Durango we

spotted our hotel for this night, the Holiday Inn on our left hand

side as we rolled by. We would be back. Off to our right we could see the charming old town Durango. That too would be revisited later this day. For right now we kept right on going up the San Juan Skyway northward toward the San Juan Mountains, a part of the Colorado Rockies.

Soon we saw flashing red lights and heard a clanging bell as a railroad crossing arm swung down halting our progress. We could see the tracks angling across the road and very soon from our right rear chugged the locomotive of the Durango Silverton Railroad puffing big black billows of smoke as it pulled several different styles of passenger cars behind it. Some of the cars were open and the passengers smiled and waved at us. We smiled and waved back. This was pleasant and fun, soon the entire train had passed, the crossing arm lifted the bell silenced and the red lights extinguished and we rolled on.

Next we came upon a glider port operated by the Durango Soaring Club. Several graceful motorless aircraft sat on the grass listing to one side and quietly sang out to us to take them aloft. The temptation was very strong, but Kari had just gotten comfortable with an aircraft held in the air by a spinning propeller attached to a running motor. Convincing her to get into an aircraft with no propeller and no motor was a far greater challenge than I was ready for right here and right now. Besides their ad slogan was a bit unnerving for a guy who flew powered aircraft for a very long time. *Enjoy the Thrill of Silent Flight* it read. Of course I knew what they were talking about, but the last thing I want in my airplane is silence while in the air. That is never a good sign. Sure, they looked graceful and pretty and serene, but next time – maybe.

The pitch of the grade increased and the road began to wind up and up passing all manner of interesting places. Right after the glider port we passed the Bueno Tempo Ranch with its riding stables. Next came the turn off for the Trimble Hot Springs to the west and the Dalton Lake Golf Course to the east. Red cliffs began showing themselves as we passed yet another golf course. We saw a sign alerting us to the presence of range cattle but we didn't see any. The elevation was getting higher and higher and for many miles there were no guard rails along the side of the road. I know it seems very odd but it is absolutely true that I a life long pilot have a deep fear of heights. I think it is contagious because Kari exhibits the exact same condition. True the scenery was stunning but totally holding Kari's attention was the sharp drop very close to her side of the car. Suddenly she let go with an outburst of stark terror. *"Road Damage!"* she shrieked and instantly pointed to the cause of this outburst. Up ahead not too far was a sign that very simply proclaimed ROAD DAMAGE. There was no further explanation, just a bald and temporarily terrifying proclamation of road damage on a narrow winding mountain road. Kari screamed and I laughed. I can't really say why I laughed, kind of a gallows laugh I'd guess but there it was. Then Kari began to laugh with me. We kept driving and whatever road damage there may have been remained happily invisibly to us.

At the Molas Pass Viewpoint we pulled off the road and stepped out of our car to enjoy some fresh mountain air and enjoy the beautiful view of the surrounding mountains and valleys and Molas Lake. Here we were within a goal post of ten thousand feet above sea level. That was very close to the altitude we had been flying at for most of this trip so far. Nearby there were majestic mountain peaks reaching upwards of 14,000 feet. At our typical flight altitude we would have flown directly into some very hard rock. Just when you think you have it under control Mother Nature shows you once again just exactly who is really in charge.

Only a little ways further up the road and actually a wee bit lower in altitude we arrived at the charming hamlet of Silverton, Colorado, year around population about 400. As with so many old western towns Silverton was the offspring of mining, mostly silver. The first significant number of settlers arrive d in Silverton between 1874 and 1875 arriving by foot and mule from as far away as China. Life was hard in those early days; just consider these statistics taken from Silverton's cemetery. Death from snow slides 117, death from miner's consumption 143, death from pneumonia 161, death from influenza 138 and death from mining accidents 202. The average annual snowfall in Silverton is 200 inches. The longest recorded period of non stop snow fall was 32 days in 1932 and to think that in our home town of Los Angeles, California it is BREAKING NEWS if it rains for more than an hour. And the growing season in Silverton lasts 14 days with rhubarb and horseradish the main crops. Given the unrelenting reality amidst this jewel of natural beauty it is no wonder that at its peak

Silverton, Colorado sported forty fully operational saloons within its petite borders.

By now Kari and I were quite hungry so we headed straight for one of those saloons cum restaurants, the Brown Bear Café. Honestly I can not tell you what exactly what we had for lunch, but I can tell you that it was abundant, delicious and reasonably priced a real *Hat Trick* for a tourist town eatery. Add to that good service delivered with a smile and a stunning polished wood and cut glass back bar that would have made Carrie Nation smile and the entire experience was a solid ten.

Gratified and satisfied we began our pleasant stroll around the century plus old mining town turned tourist destination. It offered up several cafes, at least two ice cream parlors, numerous trading posts, a smattering of trinket shops and plenty of old and historic buildings and all of this was just on Greene Street the main street of Silverton. All of this set amidst some of the most majestic scenery on earth, scenery that includes soaring snow capped mountain peaks and tall mountain pine.

SILVERTON, COLORADO

Kari and I were both totally taken by the amazing charm of

Silverton, Colorado but ostensibly we had flown here to visit

Durango. Once again the adventure was heightened and improved

by a liberal dose of serendipity. Often, not always nor in all things,

but often and in many things simply going with the spirit of the

occasion yields the best results. I was able to prove the truth of

that concept to Kari several times already on this trip and there

would be several more examples straight ahead. But for now it

was time to turn around and drive back to the great town of

Durango, Colorado.

First things first, the time had come to check into our hotel and

after five full days on the road take full advantage of the small

laundry room at the hotel. These were two simple tasks that

became a comedy of errors starting with getting in to our room.

Like virtually every hotel in the world these days the room "key" is

a plastic card with a magnetic strip that is supposed to, when properly encoded, unlock the door to our room. That is the way it is supposed to work. This is how it did work.

The young slightly frustrated counter clerk handed us our two plastic keys and Kari and I walked to our room. Upon arriving at the door I inserted my key with the only result a small red light. The door stayed locked solid. Kari then tried her key with the same result. I asked Kari if she wanted to go and get working keys or guard our bags. She chose to go and get the keys. A few minutes later she showed up with two ostensibly new keys. We again tried both keys and we got the same result; no entry. This time I went back to the front desk and by now our clerk was becoming very agitated. She muttered something about coding keys not being her task and showed a deep relief when an obviously more experienced person showed up and took over. The third time was the charm and the door opened. But the beat goes on.

Next it was critical to Kari's mental health that we establish TV contact with the Disney Channel. She actually succeeded in doing that as I began to unpack and gather up our dirty clothes for a wash. But then the TV went totally fuzzy. The audio became unbearable and the picture was only slightly discernable. So first things first we went to the laundry room and started our laundry. The only problem was there was no soap available in the laundry room. Now I don't know how things get done in Durango, Colorado but in my world commercial Laundromats typically have machines that for a fee dispense laundry detergent. Not here. Oh well even a water only wash was better than no wash at all so we went ahead with that. Next stop, back to front desk to try to get our TV back to a usable condition.

The young man who had been dispatched to our room for the purpose of repairing the television was a desk clerk, probably a bellman, but clearly only an ad hoc TV repairman. To his everlasting credit he was making an earnest if not very successful effort at repair. Our arrival had been anything but smooth and now this. Kari looked sad as she came to grips with the tragic reality that this night would be a Disney Channel free night. Fortunately Kari is not one of those people who wastes a lot of time pouting. So we went and finished up our laundry chore, took our semi clean clothes back to the room and headed out to explore Durango, Colorado.

Durango, Colorado is a very quaint and charming town in southwestern Colorado in the San Juan range of the Rocky Mountains. It grew up as a real world Wild West railroad town and rapidly became a movie star in its own right with 30 some movies having been made in and around Durango. In fact the first movie to be made in Durango was *Ticket to Tomahawk* and it was essentially a dramatized biography of the town's history. Thanks to its fairly high elevation of 6500 feet MSL even during the summer months when nearby desert towns to the west bake in triple digit misery, Durango stays fairly mild.

For many years now Durango has been mainly a tourist town drawing hikers and bikers and sightseers from the around the world. Annual events such as the Cowboy Gathering, the Railfest and the Rocky Mountain Horse Expo contribute to the tourist trade. But the true heart of Durango is its bustling historic Downtown area and it was there that Kari and I were headed. But first we would take a short river walk.

The Animas River flows from north of Silverton to a point south of Durango. It is the product of annual snow melt and it runs clear and fast. It has good fishing which we were tempted to try. That idea was nixed when we considered that we had no way to cook and eat any fish we might catch and the thought of having dead fish in our small airplane flying above the hot desert was a very serious turn off. The Animas River also has rapids and as we walked along the pathway next to the river we saw many people sail by in all manner of interesting craft, the most common of which was the good old inner tube. It looked like a lot of fun but on this day our mission was to explore downtown Durango a mere two short blocks away.

Downtown Durango, Colorado exudes the look and flavor of an old western town. It is pretty, it is charming, it is pleasant to walk through, but to me it was somewhat disappointing for its overwhelming dedication to tourism. It seemed like every other shop was a Tee shirt store. But that aside it is still a fun place to walk and see and enjoy. If Durango has a dominant focal point, other than its train station, of course, it would have to be the

majestic Victorian edifice of the Strater Hotel.

KARI IRWIN

STRATER HOTEL, DURANGO, COLORADO

The Starter Hotel has been right there at 699 Main Avenue, Durango, Colorado since 1887. I gleefully pointed out to Kari that there indeed are some things in this world older than me. She was not so sure. Everything about the place speaks of beauty and history. The walls are decorated with hand screened wall paper from Bradbury & Bradbury and the hotel claims to have the world's largest collection of walnut antique furniture. I can not verify that claim, but only a fool would dispute it. Compared to the many thousand room wonders of Las Vegas the Strater claims a far more modest 93 guest rooms, each with an authentic Victorian décor. But there is one thing the Strater can rightfully claim that no Las Vegas behemoth will ever be able to claim and that is true class. The Strater is the Queen of Durango.

Kari and I tried to enter the Diamond Belle Saloon just off the hotel lobby but the place was completely filled with happy looking folks enjoying a meal. We walked up some stairs to a mezzanine overlooking the establishment but shortly after sitting down the ever frugal Kari opined that it was too expensive and we left. Truth be told I have no idea how she formed that opinion since we hadn't even seem a menu. My guess is that just because the place looked so appealing she simply assumed that it had to be expensive. On this visit at least we would never know.

Next we discovered the box office and entrance to the Diamond Circle Melodrama Theater. Now actress Kari's eyes lit up. The temptation to buy tickets for this evening's performance was almost, but not quite overwhelming. The only problem being that we would not get back to our hotel until around 11:00 PM which would generally not be such a late hour, but with our commitment to early departures we had gotten into the habit of being sound asleep long before 11:00 PM. Rats! However her disappointment was instantly ameliorated when we were introduced to one of the actors who took us into the theater and told Kari all about the theater, the Melodrama and general information about the cast. We had just entered Kari's world and she beamed in delight. As we had so many times on this trip we again pledged to return another day and stay for the show. Our adventure just kept getting better each day. Neither of us really knew what to expect at each place we visited along the way and so far each destination brought us amazing and sensational new sights and experiences. We really will come back and we will find a way next time to bring mom. Oh boy, that will mean a whole lot of driving.

We left the Strater Hotel happy but still hungry and began walking back in the general direction of our hotel. Despite the many restaurants in Durango, many of them quite good I am told, we for whatever reason didn't find one, other than at the Strater, that grabbed us so on we walked. Shortly after we had crossed the railroad tracks we turned and watched as one of the steam locomotives of the Durango Silverton Railroad chugged by pulling its many cars. Durango really is a very cool place.

I am sad to report that with so many other options we ended up dining that night at Applebee's. Now I hasten to add that this is in no way a suggestion that Applebee's is a bad place to eat but it is a chain restaurant and we had passed up so many other more interesting options. Oh well, the meal was decent and the price was right at Applebee's.

We watched the sun set over Durango and then we returned to our hotel and our room hoping against all odds that somehow our television would miraculously work. Nope, there would be no Disney Channel for Kari this night. There was however a nice indoor swimming pool. Some kids and even some adults would have thrown a great big hissy fit at being denied their favorite television viewing for the evening but Kari just shrugged and slipped into her swimming suit. She swam for the better part of an hour as I read *Final Approach* by John Nance. By the time we left the pool it was very close to our bed time. Kari took a quick shower and soon we were both asleep. Tomorrow we would leave this charming little Colorado town and head south southwest to Gallup, New Mexico. By now we had fully adjusted to our new sleep habits; we had enjoyed a very full day of some really wonderfully fresh mountain air and had had a good meal so sleep came swift and deep.

Day Six

DRO – GUP

(Durango, CO –to- Gallup. NM)

For some odd reason our drive back to the Durango La Plata County Airport seemed much faster than our drive into Durango just yesterday.   I think that perception is caused by really liking some place. I mean when you really like some place it always seems to take far too long to get there on the one hand and it is left behind far too quickly on the other hand. Whatever the cause we soon found ourselves right back at the Durango Jet Center.

By now our preflight ritual had become ingrained and routine. First we secured our bags in the airplane. Then Kari began removing the tie down chains and taking the chocks away from our landing gear wheels. As she was doing this I was checking the fuel quantity and condition and the oil quantity and condition. Next I would clean our windshield if necessary. Then I began a slow walk about the aircraft in a counter clockwise direction starting and ending at the pilot's side door. I looked closely at the fuselage and the wings and the flight controls, moving those softly to assure that they were working properly and there was no binding. Of course I also eyeballed the tires looking for proper inflation and the absence of any potentially dangerous dings, cuts, digs or flat spots. From the back of the plane I dropped down and looked up underneath the fuselage looking for any abnormalities. I also looked over the top of the wings to just double check that the fuel caps were in the proper position. One of the many good features of the Cessna Cardinal is that it sits low enough that you can actually see the tops of the wings without using a ladder. Back at the front of the airplane I once again studied as much of the engine compartment as I could through the small inspection port and the forward openings in the cowling. I always ran my hand over the propeller feeling for any dings. Today there were none and that is precisely how it should be. A good sized ding can rapidly turn into a crack which can quickly lead to a broken propeller. Propeller tips can turn at the speed of sound. Should a portion of the propeller break off it would instantly be out of balance and that condition is capable of ripping the engine off of the airplane. Should that happen the airplane and all in it drop to the ground like a very heavy falling leaf. The conclusion of such an event is always fatal so I always check the propeller. The process also includes checking all of the numerous antennas. While the loss of two way radio communication abilities or the loss of VOR navigation aids would not very likely be fatal it is annoying and it is best if avoided. Last but by no means least I like to step back several feet from the airplane and walk around it one more time from a slight distance just giving it a careful look. Is it listing to one side? Is there some visible oddity I didn't see up close? On this bright clear southern Colorado day our magnificent Cessna Cardinal N13HK once again checked out as airworthy and in I climbed.

Our trip today would take about 1.2 hours and we would fly approximately 111 nautical miles. Our first VOR navigation aid was amusingly named the Rattlesnake VOR. We would be flying right by the fairly good sized town of Farmington, New Mexico which lies directly west of the Rattlesnake VOR. We would be departing Mesa Verde or the green mesa and from Farmington, New Mexico to Gallup New Mexico we would be over basically barren desert. Close to our track and about 40 miles south southwest of Farmington, New Mexico there is according to the United States Department of Transportation as depicted on the Denver Sectional Aeronautical Chart a Trading Post. That same aeronautical chart further revealed that we would be flying over Hunter's Wash and abeam the Chuska Mountains as we approached Gallup, New Mexico. But that trading post was truly intriguing because it seemed, by looking at the chart to be literally in the middle of nowhere. Well obviously it was somewhere, but I wondered who the trading post folks traded with. One of the fascinating ironies of America's great southwest is the fact that it has much more activity than you can imagine from merely looking at a map. You can also get a false sense to total emptiness by flying over it at 35,000 feet in a commercial jet. Our enroute altitude today would be 10,500 feet and from that altitude we would enjoy a far more revealing and interesting view than our jet brothers above us.

I started our engine and once again it leapt into operation instantly and flawlessly which is always a good sign. Next I set up both our communications radios and our navigation radios, I also fired up my trust worthy Garmin GPS and activated our route to Gallup, New Mexico, and it was actually a very simple route being a straight line directly from Durango, Colorado to Gallup, New Mexico. We had no overwhelming terrain to avoid and no restricted airspace to circumnavigate. We hadn't even left the ground and already this was looking like an easy flying day. Even my previously raging but totally irrational anxiety had waned significantly. We had reached the furthest point on our trip and we were now slowly but surely working our way back home. Even when you are having one heck of a great time as both Kari and I were in fact having, thoughts of home are always pleasing.

We announced our departure from the ramp and taxied north passed the airline terminal. It looked much less impressive from this view than it looked either inside or on the street side. We rambled on. As we approached runway 20 I stopped the airplane, set the brake and performed the routine run up. Kari had already opened the cowl flaps being the very competent co pilot that she is. Everything checked out precisely as it was suppose to check out and after making one more announcement on the radio and taking a careful look around for any other traffic we took runway 20, applied full take off power and began our take off roll. As our speed increased I saw two rabbits standing to my left on the runway completely indifferent to the noise we were making. Some one from the FAA needs to have a chat with those rule breaking rabbits. With just a slight back pressure on the yoke we lifted gently up into the sky.

The sky was crystal clear and the air was smooth as silk as we climbed to our chosen cruise altitude of 10,500 feet MSL. We could see well over a hundred miles in any direction except behind us where our visibility was interfered with by some rather tall mountains. Farmington, New Mexico came quickly into view. One thing general aviation pilots always do or at least always should do as we fly along is to constantly look for potential landing areas should landing become necessary ahead of schedule. Okay I will say it as it is, we need to always be aware of where we might have to land should that big fan out front stop turning. I am most pleased to report that so far in my 42 plus years of flying I have not once made a landing anywhere but at the chosen and intended airport. Still, it is wise to always consider all available options. The great big tower controlled airport at Farmington, New Mexico would make an excellent alternative landing field should an emergency occur. That is, of course, not the way these things happen. Pilots are necessarily interested in the Federal Aviation Regulations and to some extent even in those portions of the United States Code that control flight in the United States of America, but it is always Murphy's Law that rules everything, even flight. So a catastrophic engine failure should it happen at all would never happen right above or very near a nice big runway, it would happen if it actually did happen well out over some utterly miserable desolate terrain. Well gee whiz all of our engine gauges were indicating a superbly performing engine and the Rattlesnake VOR was coming in loud and clear so Murphy and his never ending stinking law would not impact our lives this day.

With Farmington, New Mexico moving quickly to our six o'clock

the scenery ahead rapidly became desolate indeed. Somewhere

out there was that fascinating Trading Post depicted on our chart

but darned if I could identify it on the ground beneath us. Well it

had to be there, our federal government said it was there so it really

had to be there, right?

Hunters Wash was easy to spot as were the Chuska Mountains.

Off to our right was Window Rock, Arizona the official home of

the Navajo Nation. As fascinating as it may be to visit Window

Rock, Arizona today we would simply fly right on by on our way

to Gallup, New Mexico. Here was yet another one of those "next

time" situations. The only problem is that for most of us mere

humans, next time frequently does not happen. So we motored on.

As we got closer to our destination of Gallup, New Mexico I dialed

in the automated weather information frequency for the Gallup

Municipal Airport on 118.375 and also the Unicom frequency for the Gallup Municipal Airport on 122.95. I was pleased to learn that there were only light winds and that those winds favored runway 24 meaning that our approach would essentially be straight in. Kari had been monitoring the oil temperature gauge and it had stayed well in the green the entire flight. Kari even took control of the aircraft briefly. She very capably held our heading and altitude, an important task many pilots struggle with. But after a few minutes she proclaimed, "your plane" and released her hands from the control yoke.

We were getting closer now and I started a shallow descent. Soon the airport came into sight and about at that very moment we heard a twin Cessna announce his intentions to land at the Gallup Municipal Airport. From his announcement he was about ten miles behind us, but he was a twin and so could fairly quickly close that gap. It was decision time. I was only about five miles from the airport so I decided to make a straight in approach and announced my intentions accordingly. The twin driver then announced his position and he was indeed catching up with us but I was reasonably certain he had no desire to run us over. Still and even though it was a bright sunny day I switched on our wing tip strobe lights and continued my descent on final approach. At the same time we touched down on runway 24 at the Gallup Municipal Airport, New Mexico the pilot in the Twin Cessna announced that he was overhead and would turn left to enter downwind for runway 24 at the Gallup Municipal Airport. I reported "Cardinal one three hotel kilo down and clear runway two four, Gallup" and taxied over to Gallup Flying Service.

The ramp man was wearing a hat exactly like one I owned Kari reported to me. Sure enough he was wearing a hat proclaiming that he was a Vietnam Veteran. As often happens between Vietnam Veterans there was a short and directly to the point conversation. "When and where?" I asked. "67 and 68 river delta, Army" he replied. I then offered, "Marines, 66, 67 I Corps." Having established our respective bona fides we went on about our business and shifted the conversation to flying. I can not, of course, speak for every Vietnam veteran but for myself and for pretty much all the guys I know who are real veterans of that war, nothing ticks us off more than the far too many phonies who claim veteran status. Sometimes it is laughable when you see some dude barely in his twenties claiming he is a Vietnam veteran. But the loser panhandlers falsely identifying themselves as Vietnam veterans are really annoying. Oh well, with the extended conflict in the Middle East the whole Vietnam debacle has finally lost much of its primacy.

We hadn't even finished securing N13HK when a great big Cessna 421 pulled up right next to us on the ramp. Here was the guy who had followed us in and it was no wonder he had caught up with us so quickly, he had a pair of big powerful engines pulling him

through the sky. The airplane had the logo of Med Flight an air

ambulance service. It was occurring to me by now that air

ambulances were very popular out here in the far flung towns of

the great American southwest.

Inside the Gallup Flying Service we were greeted by an obviously

seasoned citizen who brightly enquired where we had come from.

I told him that this morning we had come from Durango, Colorado

but that we originated in southern California. His eyes twinkled as

he said "Ah I learned to fly in southern California, Oxnard Army

Airfield." "What did you fly?" I asked. "T-6's mostly" he

recalled. "Went on to fly B-17's" he offered with deep pride. I

was deeply moved. Kari sensed there was something special going

on but she is just plain too young to really get it. The "it" to get is

the sad fact that our great heroes of the World War Two generation

were rapidly dying off. It wouldn't be too much longer before they all leave this earth and yet here before us was one such man, a Mister Jack Horrett, World War Two bomber pilot. Not only that but the place at which he learned to fly, the Oxnard Army Airfield is now known as the Camarillo Airport a place Kari and I visit often primarily to enjoy their locally famous tri tip sandwiches.

The nice lady behind the counter called our motel for us and was told a car would be at the airport in just a few minutes. She also relieved us of $5.35 for the over night ramp fee. She then suggested that we go next door to the airline terminal as that was the most likely place the man from the motel would look for us. I was far more accustomed to places like Los Angeles International airport, or even the much smaller but still very active Burbank airport at home. The concept of airline service at small little non towered airports like Kingman, Arizona; Durango, Colorado and now Gallup, New Mexico was only now beginning to take hold within my cranial mass. The improbable name of the airline serving both Gallup and Kingman was Great Lakes Airlines. We were very far away from the Great Lakes, yet here was the Great Lakes Airlines.

It operates mostly Beechcraft 1900 twin engine turboprop airplanes. It got its start in 1977 as Spirit Lake Airways. By 1979 it officially became incorporated as Great Lakes Aviation. Today it is a publicly traded company with headquarters in Cheyenne, Wyoming and service to numerous smaller towns and cities in the western United States. But Great Lakes Airlines even has gates at both Denver's Stapleton Airport and Chicago's O'Hara International Airport not to mention right here at the Gallup Municipal Airport.

Before we could actually get over to the "big" terminal an Indian man came in and asked for Ron Irwin. No not that kind of Indian, the kind of Indian who comes from India. Introductions were made and off we went in his Jeep. It was occurring to me that the Jeep was the vehicle of choice amongst a great many residents of America's southwest.

The Economy Inn of Gallup, New Mexico is located right on the Historic Route 66 and directly across from some frequently traveled railroad tracks. When we got to our room the first thing both Kari and I noticed were the lamp shades. They were a dark red with fringe all over them and they looked like something taken from the Munster residence. More likely they were considered the pinnacle of fashion somewhere in India. But here in Gallup, New Mexico they just looked weird and Kari and I were both giggling. Despite the fashion failure the beds seemed comfortable and most importantly there was Disney Channel on the TV. So Kari was happy despite discovering that the Economy Inn of Gallup, New Mexico did not have a swimming pool.

For the very first time on our adventure Kari's mood turned briefly dark. She has one bad habit which is to keep discomfort to her self, choosing instead to simply develop an inexplicable rotten mood. It took some digging but I eventually found out that she was having a headache. My guess was that she was most likely hungry and that pretty much any half way decent meal would resolve the problem.

We walked somewhat less than a mile in the direction we were told would take us to something approximating downtown Gallup until we found a restaurant that looked acceptable. What we had found was a very typical family style place with what turned out to be good food at a reasonable price. Kari's much more typical cheery disposition returned the instant she had food. Problem ascertained and now solved.

Sitting not far from us were two gentleman, one of them a local sheriff both enjoying coffee and conversation. At another table were at first two guys who were later joined by another man all of whom seemed to be local residents of Gallup, New Mexico. Then she appeared. She was an elderly and undeniably American Indian woman caring a tray displaying various pieces of jewelry. The sheriff and his friend were on their way out as she came in the restaurant so she went first to three gentlemen nearest to our table where she stood silently and was studiously ignored by the three men. I watched looking for any sign of interest or recognition and I saw none. I would generally have considered this snub by the locals a negative statement yet for some odd reason I welcomed what I knew would soon be her arrival at our table,

I was not to be denied; she walked next to our table and stood there quiet as a cigar store Indian until I asked her if her jewelry was from China. She proudly told us that her grandchildren made the jewelry. I could easily believe that inasmuch as none of it came remotely close to "fine" jewelry. Yet it was not bad jewelry either. In fact she had a few pieces that were rather attractive and Kari had spotted one necklace that really appealed to her. So the negotiations got under way. Taking the necklace Kari had honed in on I asked: "How much for this one?" "Ten dollars" she replied. I then opened my wallet, removed a ten dollar bill and handed it to her. That seemed to make her happy so I figured I would go to the next phase of the transaction and politely ask this amazing Navajo grandmother to offer a real Indian name for Kari. She thought a moment and then said "Bah!" I have no idea what, if anything "Bah" means in the Navajo language. I figure it probably means something like white girl sucks pickles or some such unflattering thing. But never mind, we got what we paid for, the necklace was worth ten bucks and the whole adventure was all in fun anyhow.

And this woman was a truly amazing sight with a thoroughly weathered nutmeg complexion and an overwhelmingly calm demeanor. She may or may not have been the biggest scam artist in Gallup. I really don't think that she was, but even if so just making her brief acquaintance and coming away with a pretty cool looking turquoise and something necklace was worth every penny of the ten dollars.

It was great to see Kari smiling again. So we took our time walking back towards the hotel. We did stop in a couple of Trading Posts along the way. One was operated by a couple of men of obviously Middle Eastern decent in whose establishment you really could find "native" American goods made in China. The other shop we visited was interesting but not compelling. Of course, our beloved Navajo grandma is a very hard act to follow.

By the time we got back to the hotel Kari was expressing a desire to just relax and watch TV. Our day yesterday in Silverton and Durango, Colorado ending as it did with a long walk around downtown Durango had pretty much took the stuffing out of her. Her first choice would have been to take a swim but with that option not available here a serious commitment to the Disney channel was her choice for the balance of the day. We had done one heck of a lot in only a handful of days. We were literally constantly on the go and to be completely candid Gallup, New Mexico is really not much more than a watering hole along Historic Route 66 so yeah, okay, go ahead and enjoy the Disney channel Kari. I went for a walk and found a fairly large super market.

Even at an elevation of pretty much 6500 feet MSL it was just plain hot in Gallup, New Mexico so the air conditioning in the supermarket felt great extending my stay. In all appearances this store was not very different from the Ralph's market near my home in southern California. I shopped for and ultimately purchased some bananas and a couple of other things we could eat in the morning. I looked at and considered a roasted chicken for our dinner but decided against that in favor of another restaurant meal. I would live to regret that decision.

Walking back to the motel I felt a sense of dreariness. Gallup, New Mexico just seemed kind of broken and uncared for. It had far less pizzazz than Durango, Colorado and less soul than Kayenta, Arizona. Heck even Kingman, Arizona had more energy than Gallup. But I absolutely did not feel cheated. Just meeting Jack Horrott the B-17 pilot at the airport and then our instantly beloved Navajo grandma at the restaurant made our stop at Gallup, New Mexico worthwhile. Even our budget hotel, the Economy Inn, with its strange haunted house looking lamp shades gave us a memory not to soon be forgotten. And while the Economy Inn will never pose a threat to the Ritz Carlton chain it gave us a comfortable room at a very reasonable price. There was, however, one experience in Gallup, New Mexico I really wish we had not had. That experience was our dinner.

Kari and I headed out again only this time walking the opposite direction from our morning walk. We soon came upon a restaurant that at least looked like it might be an okay eatery but then looks can be deceiving. We entered the place and found two other people inside. One was the hostess and waitress and the other was a man who apparently was the cook. There was absolutely positively no one else in the place and that alone should have scared us away. Then Kari started twitching her nose. "Yuck, cigarettes" she exclaimed. Not that I didn't believe her but I used to be a smoker. I quit about 15 years ago now but even so my many years of smoking rendered my sniffer far less sensitive certainly than that of my 11 year old unpolluted daughter. Even so it wasn't too long before I could smell what she was referring to. The cook had been smoking, probably still was in the kitchen while preparing our food. That was good reason number two for us to run and yet we stayed. We then placed our order with waitress who wrote it down and then said "You must be from out of town" which Kari and I both interpreted to mean that no one who actually lived in Gallup would come to this place. Strike three and still we stayed. However at exactly that moment we looked at each other and said simultaneously "Rocky's." Rocky's is the restaurant at the Whiteman Airport in Los Angeles, California, our home airport. Their food is generally pretty good and we eat there often. But we still like to pick on Rocky's because from time to time the place suffers from poor service. But right here and right now we both really longed for Rocky's no matter what kind of service we may have gotten.

Our food arrived and seemed edible. We in fact ate it and did not suffer any unpleasant consequences. Nevertheless we were more than happy to pay our tab and leave. Like I said, I had made a bad decision when I decided not to buy the cooked chicken at the grocery store. But then who knew?

We had been thoroughly committed and near hyper active tourists the preceding three days so having a much quieter day in Gallup, New Mexico was actually appreciated. The only thing that caused me some tiny bit of concern was a few clouds I saw off to the west of Gallup. Were they as I suspected only isolated clouds or were they the leading edge of some far more potentially troublesome weather condition. If we need to face some rain and clouds I would be delighted to file and fly an instrument flight plan. My daughter and otherwise super co-pilot was, however, terrified of clouds. Plus were we approaching a time of the year when there were fairly frequent thunderstorms in this general area.

Thunderstorms were something even I was terrified of flying in. So what did those clouds to the west mean anyhow? Well we weren't leaving tonight, so I figured we could just wait until tomorrow morning. Very soon after the sun was completely gone from view we extinguished the TV and lights and we were quickly fast asleep.

After a quick shower and shave in the morning I put on my clothes and ran outside and looked toward the west. Yep! There were still clouds in that direction. But they seemed to reach only to about the edge of town. Beyond that it looked absolutely clear as usual.

Well alright now would be an excellent time to call the flight service briefing number and get a current weather briefing for the route between Gallup, New Mexico and Sedona, Arizona. I have the telephone number for flight service on my cell phone speed dial so I punched it in, waited for the recorded answer and hit the number one button to transfer to a briefer. After about ten minutes on hold I hung up and finished packing. I then called again and again I was put on hold. Again I hung up after more than ten minutes on hold. "This is insane" I said to myself. Like all good American pilots I love throwing barbs at the FAA but they were far better at providing real flight service. Things are not always automatically better when they are taken over by private industry. That had certainly been true in this case. The FAA had transferred operation of its flight service operations to Lockheed Martin about a year or so earlier and ever since then service had steadily dropped. I almost hate to admit it but this is one time when I really would like to see the government by way of the FAA get involved again. Just imagine if I actually had to file an IFR flight plan or if the weather had been a truly serious concern? We would have been forced to just stay on the ground. As it was the clouds were widely scattered and did not seem to even exist much beyond the general Gallup area. I had options including a return to Gallup should the situation turn ugly once airborne. However, there were no major weather issues visible from the ground in Gallup. If we needed to we could easily have diverted south to Phoenix or even Tucson if necessary. I had no reason to even suspect such a diversion would be necessary but we had charts and fuel to do so if we had to. In fact we had many different options available to us. So while it was genuinely annoying to receive nothing more than permanent hold from the so called flight service people at Lockheed Martin it was not devastating. Also I knew there was a WSI terminal at the FBO and I would simply check it before we launched. So again we were okay but no thanks to the Lockheed Martin operation.

Day Seven

O kay so the Economy Inn was a very modest place but its proud owner was very service conscious which is a lot more than I can say for many of the bigger name hotels and motels around the world. Bright eyed and cheerful he transported us right back to the very same airport where he had found us. Happily our fine airplane was still there awaiting our arrival.

I did indeed check the WSI weather terminal and confirmed my suspicions that we had zero weather threat between Gallup, New Mexico and Sedona, Arizona. There was zero likelihood of any significant adverse change for at least the next four hours by which time we would have long been securely reattached to the ground. So there being no good reason to remain in Gallup, New Mexico and both Kari and I looking very much forward to our first visit ever to the world famous Sedona, Arizona we completed our preflight rituals swiftly but thoroughly and got in the airplane and fired her up.

All necessary and proper preflight procedures completed, appropriate radio calls having been made we took to runway 24, lined up with the center line and applied full power. This was the third time on this trip I took off from a runway at greater than 6000 feet above sea level. I was now finally convinced that it could be done. My next challenge is Leadville, Colorado home to the highest airport in North America checking in at 9927 feet MSL. I am thinking that you don't really fly an approach to landing there; you just fly the runway heading and watch the ground come up and grab you. But now I am ready to give it a try. First things first, I need to leave here and get to Sedona. Cardinal N13HK accelerated smoothly and we quickly rolled right passed a few prairie dogs on the runway bidding us farewell. Rabbits in Durango and prairie dogs in Gallup, what will the FAA do about all these incursions? And then we were flying.

Our flight path today would take us first along an established Federal Airway, Victor 291 to the Winslow VOR. At the Winslow VOR Victor 291 bent slightly to the left and went to Flagstaff, Arizona. Flagstaff, Arizona was not our intended destination; Sedona, Arizona was so as we crossed the Winslow VOR we would set up on Victor 264 which would take us right to Sedona. For the non-aviation community just think of a Victor Airway as a highway in the sky. So while technically incorrect you could think of Victor 291 as US Highway 291 and Victor 264 as US Highway 264. So in ground travel speak the plan would read something like, "Take US 291 west to Winslow and then get on US 264 for Sedona." No matter how you say it works out well and you will eventually get to Sedona, Arizona.

189

The terrain gradually became a little rougher as we headed west but then we were above it and not on it so it was merely of visual interest. As we approached Winslow, Arizona we saw a spectacular crater below us. I swear we saw this and that it was east of Winslow, Arizona. I emphasize this because there is a famous meteor crater west of Winslow, Arizona but I was not expecting to see a great crater right here to the east of Winslow. I quickly looked at my navigation instruments and told Kari to write down what I observed. We were 28 nautical miles (slant angle) from the Winslow VOR on the 062 degree radial. Right there we both saw a great big crater. Honest! Either that or we had been temporarily abducted by aliens. Both Kari and I confirmed each others observation. It was there alright. What a spectacular sight.

By the time we crossed Winslow, Arizona we were approximately two thirds of the way to Sedona. Today's flight was about 153 nautical miles and it would take us 1.8 hours as measured by the engine tachometer. According to our GPS our ground speed was averaging around 100 nautical miles per hour, down significantly from our other flight sectors because now we were most certainly flying directly into headwinds. As we flew right passed Winslow, Arizona we observed a small gaggle of alto cumulus clouds about 2000 feet above us. That was it, that was the totality of our enroute weather experience on this trip. It was yet another great day to fly.

As we inched towards Sedona, Arizona I saw a high ridge line directly in front of us. It seemed to be guarding the entrance to Sedona. It was to the east of Sedona and we would have to fly over it to get to our destination. That meant we would be flying directly into the leeward side of this ridge line. Mountains waves and rotors often produce exciting air movement on the leeward side of mountain ridges and I expected we would have a chance to experience that phenomenon as we got closer. Suddenly about 1000 feet beneath us and only slightly to my left appeared a blue and white low wing airplane heading exactly the opposite direction we were heading. It looked really pretty against the mostly green terrain below us. And while it might sound dangerous it in fact was not dangerous. The other aircraft was doing exactly what he needed to do; he was holding his altitude at and an odd thousand feet plus five hundred feet for his easterly direction of flight. I was also doing what the rules call for, flying at an even number of one thousand feet plus five hundred feet on my westerly path. By both of us doing what the rules call for we assured keeping an absolute minimum of one thousand feet between us. Stated more concisely he was flying at an altitude of 9,500 feet MSL east bound as I was flying at and altitude of 10,500 feet MSL west bound and in that way we kept a safe distance from each other even though we were clearly both using the same Victor airway.

Next came the expected bump. It was a solid bump but it was just one bump. I had alerted Kari to the likelihood of this event so she was ready and not startled. It was almost like Mother Nature had planned it that way to make sure all pilots arriving from the east were wide awake and preparing for their landing at the Sedona, Arizona Airport because landing at the Sedona, Arizona Airport can be quite a handful. In fact the locals refer to it as the USS Sedona, referring to the fact that its one runway sits high atop a small mesa with a sharp drop at both ends making it much like a land locked aircraft carrier. Shortly after we felt mother natures wake up call the famous red rocks of Sedona and the almost equally as famous Sedona, Arizona Airport drew sharply into view. This was going to be an interesting landing I thought as I looked down at what seemed like a 45 degree angle to the approach end of runway 21 at Sedona Airport.

As totally captivating as today's Sedona Airport truly is, especially while attempting to land at it and especially when approaching from the east I thought about its humble beginnings. The Sedona Arizona airport began in 1955. I could only imagine what it had been like on the 22nd day of September 1955 when pilot Ray Steele landed the first airplane ever on a 3700 dirt runway atop this towering mesa at what was at first called the Oak Creek Airport. It was but one year later that the Federal government deeded the property to the Yavapai County government for use as a public airport in perpetuity. By 1958 four airplanes called Sedona Airport nee' Oak Creek Airport home. In 1963 the runway grew to its present length of 5129 feet. Finally on June 27th 2007 Kari and Ron Irwin were lining up to land on Sedona Airport's runway 21.

By listening to the Unicom frequency of 123.00 MHz and by also listening to the Sedona AWOS (airport weather) frequency 118.535 MHz we determined that runway 21 was a good choice and that there was only one other aircraft in the pattern at Sedona and he would not be a factor for us and so we continued our descent straight into runway 21 announcing our position and intentions as we continued our approach.

My approach path had been rather steep but I had significantly reduced power and as I could I added the first ten degrees of flaps thereby slowing our descent rate and airspeed. Fortunately everything worked out just right and as we crossed over the numbers we were approaching a near level attitude and our airspeed was passing slowly below 80 miles per hour. The airspeed continued to bleed off as I continued to hold the airplane off of the runway. Finally as the airplane approached its stall speed I gently but firmly put the airplane in a nose up attitude and very shortly thereafter we reached ground with only a very slight "thunk" meaning I had stalled maybe a foot high. Rats! Kari would be all over me for that and then she was. I thought that under the circumstances the entire approach and landing had been pretty darn good, but my co-pilot was merciless.

We taxied to Red Rock Aviation and parked right next to another magnificent Cessna Cardinal, this one a retractable gear Cardinal. The air was cool and actually a bit heavier than we had grown accustomed to at the much higher altitudes we had been at for the past several days. Heck Sedona Airport is a mere 4830 feet above sea level. Below us was the town of Sedona and around us mainly to the north and to the east were those famous red rocks. Straight ahead of our airplane as it was now positioned on the ramp at the Sedona, Arizona Airport was Red Rock Aviation, the local FBO. We walked over to the building and entered.

Even at this fairly early hour of about 8:30 AM the place was

buzzing with activity, mainly scores of sightseeing flights were

being booked, by helicopter and fixed wing. Well gee whiz it

seems we had already had our sightseeing flight for the day so we

went to the general aviation counter and checked in. I told the nice

gentleman behind the counter that we needed eight gallons per

wing tank and one quart of 100 weight Aeroshell oil. He wrote

down our tail number and the information and then ran my credit

card to secure payment. Just to the left of the counter on the wall

was a direct line telephone to the Enterprise Rental Car agency in

Sedona, Arizona. I lifted the handset and with no dialing required

the telephone rang through and we arranged swiftly for a car. Sure

enough in just under twenty minutes a gentleman appeared at the

general aviation counter looking for me. He arrived shortly after I

had poured myself a cup of coffee so I invited him to join me and

he agreed. While sipping our coffee I learned that he had served in the United States Navy. Dang, yet another sailor found anchor in the desert. With our coffee done we took off down the Airport Road and into the town of Sedona, Arizona.

SEDONA, ARIZONA

One thing I have learned over the years is to never believe directions as given by people who work for car rental companies. I really don't think it is a conspiracy and yet without exception whenever I get directions from people at car rental companies they have always proven to at best be woefully inadequate and often just plain wrong. I was not to be disappointed this day.

Armed as we were with scant instructions we left in search of our temporary home for our two day stay in Sedona. First turning to our left upon leaving the parking lot in front of Enterprise Car Rental we drove east on Route 89A passed the Airport Road to Route 179. Upon reaching Route 179 we turned right as instructed and proceeded in a southerly direction observing a great deal of amazing scenery along the way. My point being just that no matter how this ride would turn out it was nevertheless a very enjoyable ride. We kept driving south on Route 179 for what was beginning to seem like a very long time. Soon we were far

199

removed from any visage of an inhabited area. "Where the heck is the Village of Oak Creek?" I rhetorically asked Kari. After what seemed like about ten or maybe twelve miles I figured we had somehow either missed our hotel or had made a wrong turn. Consequently I made the decision to turn back. As I learned later that day I was not more than maybe a quarter mile from a point at which I would have seen the Village of Oak Creek. I credit this error to a combination of poor directions coupled with my own lack of patience. But as I said it was a beautiful ride anyhow, so there was no harm done.

We drove back to Route 89A and this time turned to our right and drove through what I guess you could call "downtown" Sedona. It was an area of many shops, hotels, restaurants and the Pink Jeep Tour Company. We continued our drive mainly north bound not then realizing that we were heading towards Flagstaff, Arizona. Well before reaching Flagstaff, however, I realized or in any event at least formed the opinion that clearly the Village of Oak Creek did not lie in this direction either. We needed to turn around and we were both getting a little hungry so it was fortunate that a small convenience store soon appeared on our left. We turned in and got a small snack and I asked the clerk if she knew where the Village of Oak Creek was. Her reaction was as if I had just asked her for directions to Thornburi near Bangkok, Thailand. Still we were thoroughly soaking up all of the beautiful scenery and we had no pressing matters to attend to so we turned around and drove back towards "downtown" Sedona. We drove right passed the intersection with Route 179 right passed the Airport Road and right passed the Enterprise Car Rental office before giving up yet again and turned into the driveway of a building that had a sign proclaiming "Tourist Information." When we entered the office we were informed that the Tourist Information Office had moved. There is that darn Murphy and his evil law yet again. Nevertheless one of the young ladies we spoke to offered very good and thorough directions to the Village of Oak Creek. Indeed we had been going the right way on the right road and merely needed to go

just a little bit further to find the Village of Oak Creek. We

thanked her profusely and went right back the way we started only

this time I turned up the Airport Road. Kari and I were hungry

now and there was a pretty dog gone good restaurant at the Sedona

Airport. The hotel could wait; our room would not be ready just

yet anyhow.

What do Mercedes Benz and Sedona, Arizona have in common?

For a truly comprehensive look back on the development of

Sedona, Arizona as we know it today we would have to travel back

an estimated 350 million years, give or take a few million, to the

point in time when the various geological and weather processes

began to form the beautiful red rocks of Sedona. That is however

more than a bit of over kill. It is interesting to note that the first known American Indian settlers, the Hopi Indians did manage to successfully grow corn, beans and squash in a very arid place that averages a mere fifteen to twenty inches of rain a year. But apparently not all was well in paradise because the Indian population departed what is today called Sedona about 500 years ago. Next in the late 19th century came the first settler's of European origin. Population growth started slow given the remoteness of the location. Eventually there were enough folks living in the Sedona area that a post office became necessary. The first post master a Mr. T. C. Schnebly quickly named that first station Sedona after his wife. Today Sedona, Arizona has about 22,000 residents and literally hundreds of thousands of visitors annually.

Now to answer that question, both *Mercedes* Benz and *Sedona,* Arizona were named after a woman by a loving man.

Hunger solved Kari and I finally found our hotel amidst a sea of nasty road construction.

We quickly got settled in and headed straight back out for some serious sightseeing. We went back to the areas where we had seen the Pink Jeep Tours and what we had dubbed downtown Sedona and found a place to park. We walked through numerous shops including one Harley Davidson store with no motorcycles but lots of branded merchandise and a great view of the "Snoopy" red rock formation. All of the stores in one way or another had a distinctly western flavor with the emphasis on the American Indian even though the American Indian bugged out about 500 years before. There was also a fairly strong "New Age" tone through out the various shops with plenty of crystals and more than a few crystal balls on display. All in all it was essentially a mix of Melrose and Rodeo Drive with a western/Indian/New Age spin.

There was one store, however, that intrigued both Kari and me. It was the Three Dog Bakery. The food that they had there looked so good I at first thought it was a regular people bakery. In fact as the name strongly hints it is a bakery for dogs, very spoiled dogs to be sure, but dogs nonetheless. In addition to incredible looking baked goods for everyone's favorite pooches they had puppy clothes and accessories. Now this was truly a Rodeo Drive moment. Yet here it was in Sedona. I was even more stunned to learn that the Three Dog Bakery was in fact a national chain. Well it has been said by many that America really is going to the dogs. At least they were dogs with a touch of class.

By the time we had exhausted ourselves by looking at a million dream catchers, unending Tee shirts, cowboy boots and cowboy hats and all manner of Southwestern and/or Indian Art Kari and I had become once again hungry. As we walked to our rented car

Kari mentioned that we had driven by a place called Picazzo and it

looked intriguing to her. Picazzo was to the west right on Route

89A so off we went in search of Picazzo and then there it was.

What a great pizza joint! We split our pizza with one half being a

"Vortex" and the other half being something a bit more pedestrian

like sausage. It was all excellent, a real treat, a meal we truly and

thoroughly enjoyed. To our never ending joy not only was the

pizza excellent but the cost was reasonable as well. Great food and

a good price is a combination very hard to beat. Kari and I both

gave Picazzo's five stars. Oh we aren't restaurant critics but that

didn't stop us.

It was starting to get well into the evening and even though we

were not flying tomorrow our sleep schedule on this trip made us get tired ahead of schedule. So after our great pizza we started back in the direction of our hotel. However not far from our hotel was an outlet mall so we stopped in there first in search of a book store. We did find a bookstore attractively named "The Worm." I was definitely not browsing, I had a very specific item in mind, I wanted and quickly found a booked entitled *The Saboteurs* by W.E,B. Griffin. Having found and paid for my book we then did some browsing and came upon a display of Navajo flutes. The Navajo flute is made of wood and has a rich throaty haunting sound. Kari looked at the flutes and held one. Her eyes lit up with anticipation but she said nothing. This was actually the beginning of a rather amusing sub plot to our overall adventure. The price marked for the flute was $39.00, not a bad price I thought knowing absolutely nothing about Navajo flutes. But for some inexplicable reason we were not moved to buy that one and we left the store with my novel in hand.

Nearby we came upon yet another Indian trinket shop and went in. The clerk was a pleasant young man who we quickly learned was a violin player. Kari and I immediately dubbed him "violin man." He too had a Navajo flute and it looked similar to the one we had seen at the book store only his Navajo flute was offered at $69.00. I just had to ask him how it was that his flute was nearly twice the price of the one a few doors down. To his everlasting credit he gave a genuinely honest answer. "I really don't know" he said first. It is sadly so rare for anyone to flat out admit that they don't know something and frequently it is the most truthful answer and one I can respect. He then quickly added that there are different woods and manufacturing techniques that result in different sound quality. That seemed reasonable and I very much respected what I saw as a fair and genuine answer. "Violin Man" had gained my respect but we would not buy the flute, not this one, not now. We had one more day in Sedona and his shop was very close to our hotel. Sometime tomorrow perhaps we would return and buy the flute. That too did not happen and the plot thickens. There were two things about this entire series of events that deserve a quick mention. First was that I was willing to pay significantly more for the second flute solely on the basis of "Violin Man's" candid conversation. It was not that the book store clerk was in anyway dishonest; in fact we simply never discussed the flute with him. It was just that I deeply appreciate folks who talk straight and Violin Man had done that. The other interesting point was that Kari not once whined or complained or demanded a flute. She accepted the whole thing in good grace and with a smile. I know from years of experience that such mature behavior from an 11 year old is a rare and wonderful thing. But then again maybe she knew from her 11 years of experience that sooner or later she would not be denied. And so the story continues.

Kari performed her nightly ritual of swimming followed by shower followed by Disney Channel followed by sleep. The swimming took place as we enjoyed a spectacular sunset over the red rocks of Sedona. It really doesn't get much better than this. There really is so much beauty in the American southwest. It made me think of a history teacher I had in high school way back a very long time ago. I can not now recall his name but I do recall he was a native of Arizona and a true fan. He used to bring copies of his favorite magazine, *Arizona Highways,* into school for his students to enjoy. He really was a hard core Arizona booster. Who knows he may well be retired and living nearby where we were at this very moment. But as teenagers tend to be I was brain dead back then and I saw only cactus and sand in Arizona. Boy was I ever wrong. After this trip I am certain Kari will not make that same mistake. Thank you sir, whatever your name, for at least trying to enlighten me.

Day Eight - Sedona. AZ No flight

For the very first time since leaving the Whiteman Airport back in Los Angeles we had no flight scheduled for this day. So we allowed ourselves a little extra sack time arising about 7:30 AM. That actually felt real good. We had also pretty much burned out on the commercial glitz of Sedona and wanted to spend at least some time this day enjoying more of its incredible natural beauty and charm. So after a light breakfast as usual we drove over to the base of Bell Rock, parked the car and began to hike the trail that circumnavigates this amazing edifice.

The sun was rapidly warming the air and we knew that in only a few hours it would become unpleasantly hot. But right now it was just right and frankly the path we chose was not very challenging being mostly level. Still we committed to at least a one hour hike which meant we would cover more than three miles, a decent little work out. Red rock, scrub and cactus were everywhere. From time to time a mountain biker would pass us by but on this day for this trip we were the sole hikers. It was an hour of mostly serenity. We saw an occasional bird but nothing else from the animal world except as I said a couple of mountain bikers. The deep red rock glowed against a rich blue sky and the entire scene was accented with green plants and bright yellow/green cactus. It was very much as if we were walking inside a beautiful oil painting of the southwest; it was surreal.

Kari and I talked about how we, her and her mom and I would often walk around the trails in Coldwater Canyon back home and how despite the beauty of that area this was just so much more impressive. We agreed that we really needed to find a way to bring mom here. We both knew she would love the experience once we actually got her here. Mom is an adorable but stubborn woman.

STUNNING ARIZONA CACTUS

Our walk complete in just a wee bit more than an hour it was time

for a driving tour. We took Route 179 to the now familiar Route

89A and took that road west to the town of Cottonwood, Arizona about 17 miles from Sedona. The drive took us through pastoral lands with rolling hills.

Cottonwood, Arizona was formally established in 1879 and became a farming community. It was also a great place to hunt both rabbit and quail. Cottonwood developed a reputation for lawlessness as many of its early citizens had been run out of nearby towns. During the Prohibition era Cottonwood, Arizona was also a bootlegger's center. Today Cottonwood, Arizona is a quiet modest town with a population just over 10,000 and a quaint Old Town area with an attractive old west flavor. Cottonwood is unlikely to ever challenge Sedona as a tourist destination but it is definitely worthy of a day trip and it is a nice reprieve from the runaway commercialism of Sedona.

On our drive back to Sedona we took Red Rock Loop Road which loops around as the name suggests and exposes you to many views not seen from the main highway. It also took us through a rural residential area and about 30% of the road is unpaved making for a more interesting drive.

But among other things today we had been told by the waitress at the small Italian restaurant where had enjoyed a quick lunch that many better deals on Indian items could be found at the relatively nearby Flagstaff, Arizona so off we went this time heading north bound on Highway 89A.

The somewhat bland sounding Highway 89A is also called Oak Creek Canyon Drive and it is absolutely gorgeous. Leaving the immediate Sedona area we passed the country store we had visited the previous day and then continued eventually passing Slide Rock

State Park where it is possible to stay cool by enjoying naturally created water slides. Oddly Kari expressed a lack of interest in Slide Rock State Park so we continued on towards Flagstaff initially under a canopy of trees. There was an interesting stream off of the road and we passed several campgrounds, all very busy with campers. The road winds itself along through mountainous terrain as we gained elevation from the low four thousand foot level in Sedona to eventually the almost seven thousand foot level in Flagstaff, Arizona.

One sight we saw was truly odd. As we were ascending up Oak Creek Canyon Drive descending and coming from the Flagstaff area were three guys on bicycles. But wait they sure are sitting high and those sure are strange looking bicycles I observed. Wait a bleeping minute, those aren't bicycles, those are unicycles. Wow! Kari and I watched in amazement as we drove by three happy looking guys riding blissfully down a magnificent mountain road on unicycles. That was indeed, truly odd.

We arrived in the greater Flagstaff area in pretty close to one hour's time. I noticed that the airport was nearby and I wanted to visit it at least briefly because it had originally been on our list of stops. Also a friend of mine regularly flew his Cardinal out of the Flagstaff Airport to the Whiteman Airport in Los Angeles, California. However he had somewhat of a hot rod Cardinal. It was a retractable gear Cardinal but beyond that he had had his Cardinal turbo charged. That meant that he could now fly his Cardinal well into the flight levels, above eighteen thousand feet any time he so desired. I could only imagine the reaction of the airline pilots upon hearing him on the radio. "L.A. Center, Cardinal one two three level at flight level two zero zero" he might say. "Did he just say CARDINAL in the flight levels" might well exclaim an airline pilot on the same frequency. He had to have a great time with his high flying Cardinal hot rod. But today his Cardinal was not their or at least was not within our view so we continued on into Flagstaff, Arizona.

It seems that our old friend from Kingman, Arizona, Lieutenant Beale had arrived in what was to become Flagstaff in 1855, about two years before he got to Kingman, Arizona. The first known permanent resident of Flagstaff, Arizona Territory built a small house on the west side of town in 1876. His name was Thomas F. McMillan. In 1884 Flagstaff, Arizona came to the attention of Astronomer Percival Lowell who was searching for clear skies through which to observe the stars and planets beyond. Within a couple of years the now famous Lowell Observatory was built and a custom designed 24 inch telescope was installed. More than three decades later the planet Pluto was discovered using one of the observatory's telescopes. Flagstaff has also gained in fame and stature with both its symphony orchestra and Northern Arizona

University formerly known as Northern Arizona Normal School.
As so often happens with what we call progress the original
downtown areas of Flagstaff began to crumble as major businesses
moved out. There has however been a renaissance in downtown
Flagstaff and that is a good thing because that was our destination.
And this is where our quest for a Navajo flute rejoins our story.

We parked our rental car and walked briskly to the very first store
that looked as if it might have Navajo flutes in stock. It did not.
But the clerk said: "Ah, you need to see Kelly. His store is across
the street; it's called Sacred Rites." Our next stop was therefore a
small shop called Sacred Rites.

It was instantly identifiable as a New Age palace. It had more
Buddha images than most stores in Bangkok. There were crystals
everywhere and there was the smiling owner a Mister Kelly

McCabe, a fifty or maybe even sixty something hippie with long

gray hair and an impish smile. You can't help but to like this guy

Kelly McCabe. We mentioned the Navajo flute and faster than

you can say: "Every good boy deserves fudge" one appeared in the

capable hands of Mr. Kelly McCabe. Kari's eyes and ears were

riveted to Mr. Kelly McCabe who promptly demonstrated exactly

how the Navajo flute should be played. He was good, very good.

Kari was impressed, very impressed. Next Mr. Kelly McCabe

showed us a whole array of Navajo flutes ranging from as little as

$89.00 to several hundred dollars. He has a magic about him Mr.

Kelly McCabe because I knew immediately that I was about to

spend $89 on a Navajo flute. I had walked away from a $39.00

Navajo flute and quibbled a bit with "Violin Man" about a $69.00

Navajo flute, but here was the amazing Mr. Kelly McCabe about to

relieve me of $89.00 for a Navajo flute, with no feathers. It did

sound good though. Kari's first efforts were as to be expected, not

very well. "When you leak you squeak" said the knowledgeable

Mr. Kelly McCabe concurrently showing the deeply impressed

Kari Irwin proper fingering action on the Navajo flute. The squeaks would continue, of course, but the flute was rapidly hers to learn on. Mission accomplished we left the establishment of Mr. Kelly McCabe but not before also purchasing a copy of his music CD entitled *Sacred Rites Sacred Flute*.

Now I needed an instrument, something suited to my astoundingly minimal musical talents. We entered a nearby store and soon found the perfect answer for dear old dad. It really is a nice looking thing, my Navajo rattle. And it rattles really well. More importantly it was perfectly suited to my musical level. Yes even I can shake it more or less rhythmically. And so we formed our band: *Geezer and the Kid*. Now it is sadly true that Hell will host the Stanley Cup Playoffs long before Kari and I will ever be signed to a record deal. But so darn what! We were already having a first class blast tooting and squeaking and rattling our way through beautiful downtown Flagstaff, Arizona. Mission accomplished we headed back to Sedona.

Kari kept working on that Navajo flute almost all the way back to Sedona, and no it didn't bother me. Heck three quarters of the notes were fine. It was only twenty five per cent squeaking. I was just happy to see her deep enthusiasm.

Already we had enjoyed a very full day. We had taken an early morning hike followed by a road trip to Cottonwood, Arizona, then a side trip around Red Rock Loop and finally a wonderful road trip up to Flagstaff, Arizona. But in some ways the best was yet to come. Maybe I was finally starting to crack from all of the exposure but all at once I wanted some cool Indian stuff for me. Whatever it was I turned into the parking area of yet one more

Trading Post, this one called the Raven's Nest on good old Arizona Highway 89A right by the Airport Road.

Inside the small shop a slender man wearing a black Tee shirt emblazoned with *STURGIS*. Clearly a motorcycle enthusiast I thought to myself. Behind him was a large mostly green but accented in bright red and yellow was a tweak beaked parrot sitting on his perch. The tweaked beak I ultimately learned was a birth defect. The motorcycle man was assisting a customer so Kari and I began perusing the many interesting items on display. Soon the other customer left the store and he turned his attention to us. His name was Bob Colony and he came to Sedona several years ago now from Burbank, California, our home town. When he lived in Burbank, California he owned and operated a store called The Vanishing Indian which was still in business in Burbank. Yes indeed he was a motorcycle enthusiast with a very nice Harley Davidson motorcycle. He was also a full blooded Apache Indian.

Bob Colony was a full blooded Apache! What happened to names like Geronimo? Oh well who was I to doubt him. Bob also busied himself by nursing abused and abandoned animals back to health a fact that explained among other things how he came to have a parrot with a tweaked beak. Also in my opinion Bob Colony was an interesting and pleasant guy. Kari had already spotted a necklace that was destined to become hers. Now least you form the very incorrect opinion that my daughter is one of those materialistic spoiled brat types, the necklace she liked cost $3.50. We also learned from Bob Colony that the necklace we bought from the Navajo grandma in Gallup, New Mexico was indeed authentic Navajo, well made with real turquoise and worth every penny of the mere ten bucks we had paid for it. Well what do you know about that, we made a real deal.

Then I spotted a ring that was perfect and it cost far less than similar rings I had spotted along the way on our adventure. It was a very handsome ring decorated with turquoise and coral. Bob also then explained how Indians came into possession of Coral. The answer was simple enough, they traded for it. He also explained that all or almost all Indian jewelry with stones had a soft material sometimes just paper beneath the stones to cushion them. It was therefore a very bad idea to get this jewelry wet for the moisture would swell the base material and pop out the stones. I am willing to bet the price of that ring that most folks who buy this jewelry don't know this information. I was glad to learn it before I went and jumped in the swimming pool with my new ring.

Now I am really not a huge jewelry guy but my eye next caught something I simply could not avoid. It was an old silver bracelet with a Thunderbird carved on it. Come on, a pilot ignore a Thunderbird bracelet - impossible! Not only that but it was from the early 1940's so it was something that actually predates me. Bob Colony went on to explain that it was almost certainly Harvey House jewelry. Suddenly my mind drifted back to the Harvey

House railroad museum in Barstow and the El Tovar, originally a Harvey House in Grand Canyon. It seems that the Harvey House folks commissioned a great deal of Indian jewelry to sell in their stores all along the rail routes of the American southwest. Add it all up and I just had to own this piece of silver history.

That's it. We came, we saw, we chatted, we bought and now it was time for us to leave. Before we could go Bob made one more great suggestion. "You might want to go to the Airport Restaurant" he said adding that "it is Thursday night and that means it is all you can eat crab night." Kari, who dearly loves crab, lit up like Times Square. There was no doubt; we were on our way to the Airport Restaurant. Thanks Bob, that was a great suggestion and we really enjoyed our visit to your shop.

Obviously the Thursday night all you can eat crab special at the Sedona Airport Restaurant was both well known and well attended. Being as we were without a reservation we were lucky to get a table outside. There were no tables available inside. That was fine with us as the midday heat was already dissipating and we were actually quite comfortable. As promised the crab was nonstop and delicious. Clearly we decided, the Sedona Airport Restaurant is the king of airport restaurants. Man that crab was good. Eventually we were at our personal limit and it was time to go.

As we started to leave the restaurant we saw hundreds of people at the viewing point up on the Airport Road awaiting the soon to happen sunset over Sedona. In fact as I glanced around the many rims and rocks I found hundreds more people paying silent homage to the magnificent sunset. It was clear that people came literally from all points on this great earth just to experience the great event about to take place amidst the red rocks of Sedona. And here we were, just two travelers thrust basically by happenstance into this great but daily event. Sometimes the only word that can even come close to expressing the emotions of such a moment is the simple, wow! Kari and I had been blessed with a whole lot of wows since lifting off of the Whiteman Airport in Los Angeles, California a mere eight days ago.

On our way back to the hotel we discussed maybe stopping by and saying hello to Violin Man, but why? What could we say? After all we had taken his business all the way to Flagstaff and had even paid more for the privilege. Not only that but his store was already closed for the evening. We just headed to our temporary home and Kari one more time got in her evening swim.

Thinking back on it, it was truly amazing how much we had seen and done not only in our two days in Sedona but all along our entire route. There was truly no way we could have done anything even remotely like what we had done if we had been limited solely to ground transportation. There was no question but that our humble airplane made a much bigger impact than even I had at first imagined. Tomorrow we would fly on to Bullhead City, Arizona and then call the River Palms Resort Casino for a van ride across the river and into Laughlin, Nevada. But for the hour and a half airplane ride tomorrow would be a very relaxed day before our final flight back home. It would be hot, very hot in Laughlin, Nevada but then those casino air conditioners work about like a polar ice cap.

This day was now officially done. We had been to so many interesting places, done all sorts of interesting things and met several really interesting people. We were truly but cheerfully spent. Good night!

Day Nine

SEZ – IFP

(Sedona, AZ –to- Bullhead City, AZ)

A mazingly we had no trouble getting up at 5:45 AM despite the previously exhausting day. By now our routine was down to clock work precision. Getting to the airport was even easier than we thought it might be. Driving as we did for the last time, at least on this trip, passed Bell Rock and so many of the other beautiful sights that surround Sedona, Arizona made us a little bit sad to leave, but happy at the many joyous memories we were taking with us. Like Grand Canyon and Kayenta and Monument Valley and Durango and Silverton before we pledged to return here too, to beautiful Sedona, Arizona.

We would be cursed with only a tiny sprinkle of Murphy's Law at the Sedona Airport. It seems they forgot to oil and fuel the airplane. Not only that the guy attending to matters at this early hour had no record of me paying for fuel and oil. Well we could have just left and we probably would have made Bullhead City just fine, but I just can not accept the word "probably" when it comes to flight, so I ordered fuel to be pumped into our wing tanks. As that was being done I added one quart of oil to the engine and then we all went back in to the FBO terminal building. After a wee bit more digging our friendly attendant found the fuel ticket that confirmed that I had indeed paid for both the aviation gasoline and the oil the day of our arrival. All smiles now we bid farewell to Red Rock Aviation and strolled out to Cessna Cardinal N13HK. Like I said this was but a very minor application of Murphy's Law. Good.

Of course we did a thorough preflight inspection as usual but for some happy reason everything just felt perfect today as well. Just to be sure and to the total embarrassment of my poor daughter, I took my Navajo rattle and "blessed" the airplane. Clearly there was absolutely nothing that could go wrong now *said Amelia Earhart to her navigator before flying off from their last South Pacific stop and into oblivion.*

Our flight today would take us approximately 138 Nautical Miles almost due west. Okay our track was 266 degrees magnetic. But however you looked at it, it would all be pretty much over rock. We would fly just a wee bit to the north side of Prescott, Arizona and some distance on we would fly just a wee bit to the south of Kingman, Arizona. In between it can best be described as a get me there flight because there really is not much in the way of interesting sights to see, at least not looking down. Looking up, however we did contrails from some high flying jets. Kari immediately said "pressurized cabin." At some point on our trip we had seen contrails and I mentioned to her that to get to that altitude with a passenger carrying airplane it was necessary to pressurize the cabin so the pilots and passengers could breathe adequately and not succumb to hypoxia. She sucked in all of that knowledge and now every time she saw contrails she would say "pressurized cabin." She also let it be known that as much as she was enjoying all this flying around she would be much happier if I could just buy an airplane with a pressurized cabin. Kids.

We droned on and after awhile we could see Kingman, Arizona at about our one to two o'clock. I tuned in the Kingman common traffic advisory frequency on 122.8 MHz and soon we could hear mainly all the Sheble traffic taking full advantage of the relatively smooth and cool air that was here now but which would soon be gone as the sun rapidly heated the terrain beneath us. I also dialed in the Kingman VOR on 108.8 MHz and watched as the DME (Distance Measuring Equipment) began to tick off the miles. There are so many ways to keep connected with your position in the sky these days that it seems almost impossible, at least over the lower 48 of these United States to get lost and yet from time to time folks do get lost. We have the VOR, we have good old fashioned pilotage whereby you match what you see on the ground to what is depicted on the chart and in our Cardinal we actually have a still functioning LORAN and a GPS. All of that can be further supplemented with dead reckoning, a procedure by which you use time and distance calculations to estimate your position. I think you almost have to want to get lost. That having been said I would get just a wee bit disoriented on our next and final flight of this adventure. But more on that then, for now we knew exactly where we were and right now we were over Sacramento Valley heading for the Black Mountains.

As we crested the Black Mountains we called the Bullhead Tower on 123.9 and reported our position and intentions to land at the Bullhead City Airport. A Sheble Cessna was doing touch and goes and an Ameriflight Twin Beechcraft was in bound as well. This was not exactly LAX. I was told to cross over the airport mid field and make right downwind for runway 16 at the Bullhead City Airport. The temperature was already rising in our cockpit as we began our descent and we were both in a very mellow mood so I was tempted to just say to the tower, "okay." But somehow I held it together and replied with a crisp, "WILCO one three hotel kilo."

We over flew the airport as directed and almost immediately thereafter we were over the Colorado River. We were now down to only about 1700 feet and the boat traffic on the river was plainly seen. We turned to the down wind and the tower cleared us to land number two behind the Twin Beech. Eagle eyed Kari spotted the other aircraft first as it made its turn to final. She then pointed it out me and I reported it in sight and we were still cleared to land. For the very first time on this entire trip we would descend below 1000 feet MSL, the Bullhead City airport being a mere 695 feet above sea level. This change in topography really makes a difference and it resulted not only in a very smooth landing but also a very short roll out after the landing. Dang that felt good.

Straight across from the airport we could see all of the nice big hotel casinos on the Nevada side of the Colorado River. Almost immediately after we had shut down our engine a man arrived in a golf cart to take us to the FBO terminal. It was not very far away but we really did appreciate the ride in the rapidly rising heat. Once at the terminal the shuttle from the River Palms Hotel and Casino was summoned and I took care of the usual stuff including arranging for our airplane to be topped off for our longest and final flight tomorrow. We didn't have to wait long for the shuttle; I guess they want folks to get to those slot machines and table games just as fast as possible.

It is not all that difficult to imagine Laughlin, Nevada as it had once been for millions of years. It was and indeed still is blistering hot with summer temperatures frequently topping 120 degrees and arid with average annual rainfall in the 3 to 5 inch range. The Colorado River does, however, bring life to the area including lizards, rattlesnakes jack rabbits, coyotes and sometimes desert big horn sheep.

Man first arrived to this hostile area sometime three to four thousand years ago leaving petroglyphs and rock drawings to mark their existence. The first Indians in the region were the Patayans, meaning *ancient ones*. Eventually they split into Haulpai and Mojave Tribes. The early Patayans were more nomadic than the later Mojaves who engaged in agriculture along the banks of the Colorado River between what is today Hoover Dam and south to Blythe, California. Interestingly the Indian word "Mojave" means *people who live by water*. I find that fascinating given the nature of the Mojave Desert we had flown over only about eight days earlier.

Spanish explorer Melchi Diaz was arguably the first European person to visit the area now known as Laughlin, Nevada, arriving in 1540. By the 1800's there were actually paddle wheeled steamboats traveling from Bullhead City down through the Gulf of California and up the Pacific Coast to San Francisco. By 1857 our now good friend and U.S. Army camel driver, Lieutenant Edward Beale of both Flagstaff, Arizona and Kingman, Arizona fame arrived and established Fort Mojave near modern day Bullhead City. For awhile the mail was actually delivered by camel in what is now called Mojave County. That had to be a sight to see.

Next to bring growth and a bit of prosperity to this hot forsaken area was mining. That continued for about fifty years before the mines basically petered out. By 1935 the Hoover dam some 67 miles to the north was completed. The next project was the construction of Davis Dam a mere two miles upstream from Bullhead City, Arizona.

But once the major construction work was done the population of Bullhead City, Arizona and what was then called South Pointe, Nevada (today Laughlin) dropped to almost ghost town levels. Then came Don Laughlin.

Don Laughlin visited the area and was intrigued enough to purchase a boarded up motel and 6.5 acres of riverfront property for a trifling quarter million dollars. That was back in 1964 you can just make a wild guess what that property would bring today. Much as early Las Vegas had, early Laughlin, Nevada had a humble beginning when just two years later Don Laughlin's Riverside Resort had a meager 12 slot machines and 2 gaming tables and drew folks in with an all you can eat chicken dinner for

98 cents. But for some reason this lesser cousin to nearby Las Vegas continued to grow and prosper. Indeed my own father who left his home in Oak Park, Illinois in the 1970's and moved to Las Vegas, Nevada to escape the harsh Midwestern winters, used to enjoy Laughlin far more than Las Vegas. Dad was certainly not alone as any visit to modern Laughlin, Nevada will attest. Now here I was with my sweet daughter Kari Irwin.

I can assure you that walking into the River Palms or any of the other major Laughlin, Nevada hotel casinos just does not conjure up visions of ancient Indians or rattlesnakes or, except maybe for the Colorado Belle, paddle wheel steam boats. It is all a cacophony of multi colored lights and subdued sounds, punctuated occasional shrieks of joy typically by happy players from a craps table cast upon an endless sea of plush carpeting and all bathed in very efficient air conditioning. Honestly it felt good, very good after so many days out on the range. Yessiree pardner.

Even though it was still early in the morning we were given a room straight away and off we went to drop our bags and quickly freshen up. Next it was back down stairs and out for a walk along the river. Maybe we would catch a Jet Ski ride, or maybe a water skiing opportunity would come up. Well that didn't happen but for just a few dollars we did climb aboard a river taxi. It took us first back down south of the River Palms to Harrah's and then back up to the Riverfront hotel. By the time we arrived at the Riverfront it was probably already one hundred degrees so we were in no hurry to leave. We stopped at a video game arcade and I gave Kari a few dollars to have some fun with. I am always amazed by the laws that encourage minors to simply give money away on games the playing of which will never result in any significant material benefit to the child while at the same time prohibiting minors from playing let's say a slot machine which has at least some slim hope of being beneficial. Sorry I just don't get it. But it really doesn't matter and Kari was having a total blast. She was having fun so I was having fun and we were both staying cool. All was well in the universe. But Kari is a frugal girl so it was time to move on. But next before us emerged a movie theater right there in the casino complex. One of the movies showing was a Pixar Disney animation about a rat who becomes a Parisian chef. Ridiculous but per all the hype we had been seeing on Kari's devoted watching of the Disney channel we decided it was worth our time.

Yeah it had its cute and fun elements but somehow I just couldn't get all that enthused about a bunch of French sewer rats fixing dinner. Still, as I said it had its redeeming moments and it did keep us both entertained and cool for just a little bit shy of two hours.

This was a totally different kind of entertainment from what we had been enjoying over the preceding eight days but hey we needed a break. It was, however, now our lunch time.

We managed to grudgingly handle the heat as we walked to the Colorado Belle eventually landing in the Paddlewheel Restaurant. It was in this very restaurant that I had a steak with my older daughter and Kari's sister Kimberly when we had flown out here to celebrate my birthday four or maybe five years earlier. Back then the smaller airplanes would taxi up and down the face of a cliff from the runway on top. It was then easy to just walk over to river taxi and float across to Nevada. Watching the airplanes with Kimberly while enjoying my birthday lunch was a big part of the fun and all of that was gone now. Now we little guys had to park on top along with everyone else and that meant a less convenient and absolutely less fun ride in a hotel van. Oh well, in memory of better times airport wise today I enjoyed a steak with my youngest daughter, Kari.

After our meal we cruised the casinos and gift shops all in an effort to stay cool while immersed in 120 degree heat outside. Slowly but surely we worked our way back to the River Palms Hotel and Casino. Man it was HOT! We visited a couple more gift shops that were not all that interesting. I did buy a deck of "real" casino playing cards for my daughter Kimberly who was in school learning how to be a professionally dealer. But other than that our only activity at this peak period of the heat was avoiding the heat. Then I discovered to my chagrin that I had something important to do.

Kari and I went back to our room and I looked for my electric razor. Where the heck was my electric razor anyhow? I only had two small bags it wouldn't take long to search them both. I did search them both and there was no electric razor. This quickly became a huge concern to me because I just can not stand facial stubble. I can never be a true Hollywood stud muffin I know, but sorry I just can't handle the itchy nasty feeling of fuzz on my face.

Something had to be done and done now. That something was

obviously to buy a new razor, but where? It is the but where part

of all this that makes it interesting. Why? Because for all of the

glitz and glamour of all these multi million dollar hotel casinos, for

all the millions upon millions of dollars invested in slot machines

and green felt gaming tables and despite all of the millions of

dollars played on them, in the end Laughlin, Nevada has nothing

practical. Sure you can get a $300 facial, or a diamond encrusted

toothpick or a case of some really good scotch, but you can't get a

razor. No really unless you steal it from another hotel guest you

can not get a razor in Laughlin, Nevada. In fact Laughlin, Nevada

offers virtually none of the practical needs like groceries for

example or casual clothing beyond casino souvenir stuff.

Absolutely Laughlin, Nevada has no electric razor. Yeah sure

there were some el cheapo blade razors in the gift shop but I hadn't

used a blade razor in forty years. I'd look like the goalie for the

Harvard dart team if I tried that. No thanks.

So I did the one thing you have to do when you really need something, anything at even a moderately decent hotel, I went and had a chat with the Bell Captain. The driver was out on a run but would be back in twenty minutes. Then the driver would take me into Bullhead City, Arizona where all the practical stuff for Laughlin came from and I could buy a new electric razor. Whew! He came, we went, job done.

Yeah okay so this is not up there with cliff hanging in flight emergencies or hair raising encounters with angry Indians but at the end of the day it was a part of the total experience and it is truly amazing to me that flashy Laughlin, Nevada has such a total absence of necessary products. Heck even Las Vegas has a Wal Mart. Well it does, doesn't it?

It was getting close to that time of day when Kari needed her swim. But first we stopped by Pasta Cucina a fairly small and charming in house Italian Restaurant at the River Palms. Our meal was fine and it was time to swim.

The sun was low on the horizon by the time we reached the swimming pool. Still it was plenty warm and the pool was amazingly crowded. Yes it was a large swimming pool in fact it was a very large swimming pool but it was over run with the human condition. Kari would not be denied. In she went. Still with such an overload it was not fun and we didn't stay very long.

Back in the room she took her last shower on the road and we chatted a little bit about everything we had seen and done on this fantastic journey. We both instantly agreed that for reasons not completely explainable the modest town of Kayenta, Arizona,

Navajo Nation had been our favorite place. This was not, however, to take anything away from Grand Canyon or Durango or Silverton or Sedona. In fact even less enjoyable but still interesting Barstow – Daggett and even Kingman, Arizona had their interesting aspects Kari admitted. She was adamant, however, about Gallup, New Mexico. That place she said with conviction could very easily be forgotten. Well she had a point but I did indeed find things of interest there not the least of which was our adopted Navajo grandma who as it turned out had given us a great deal on a nice Indian necklace. But kids and adults see things differently. That will never change in the history of man.

We also both agreed that we had had one heck of a great time and a very real adventure. Tomorrow we would arrive back home but we would never ever be the same as we were when we had left. We would forever carry vivid memories of our many adventures along the way on this fantastic father daughter joint venture. We were both completely surprised by the amazing Monument Valley. Our partial circumnavigation of Bell Rock in Sedona had its own special magic. Even the relatively speaking mundane Peggy Sue's Nifty Fifty's Diner would never be completely forgotten. And Kari was very appreciative of her modest jewelry acquisitions. In the acquisition department number one was by far her Navajo flute with which she now entertained me. It was sweet. Tomorrow this adventure would end but it was clear that the memories we shared would go on forever.

We watched local news before going to bed and saw a Piper Arrow flattened and off to the side of the runway at Henderson, Nevada. The reporter told us that the airplane had come from Van Nuys, California earlier today. Heck that airport, Van Nuys, is less than five miles from the Whiteman Airport. If there was any good news in all of this there had been no reports of any serious injuries. That is always a great thing. I not could help but to wonder what had happened; I always do. One thing for sure, it was my duty to get Kari and I safely back home tomorrow and without making the local news anywhere along the way. Doing that successfully would require rest. "Good night Kari." "Good night daddy and thanks."

Day Ten

IFP – WHP

(Bullhead, AZ – to – Whiteman Airport, Los Angeles, CA)

W e had talked to Nenita, Kari's mom and my bride, last night and told her we would be landing at the Whiteman Airport at 9:30 AM. Now the pressure was on to arrive on schedule. If we wanted to be late we could have taken a regular airline, but by golly we were going to arrive on time. So by 6:30 AM we were in the hotel van on our way to the Bullhead City Airport just across the Colorado River. The Casino area was strangely quiet at this hour but out front the activity was bustling. We were coming up on the 4th of July weekend and there were lot's of folks already arriving to enjoy the huge fireworks display. We were sorry we would miss it but try as you may you can't always be everywhere and do everything. The air was already warm and rapidly approaching hot. That particular element of Laughlin, Nevada we would absolutely not miss.

We stopped by the FBO at the Bullhead City Airport and settled up for our fuel. I had left my laptop computer there as well not wanting to schlep it to and from the hotel. It was right where it was supposed be so I retrieved it and we walked out to the ramp and our mighty aircraft Cardinal N13HK. Barring any highly unusual winds our flight time to Whiteman would be right about two hours and it was only a few minutes after 7:00 AM so we took our time in our loading and preflight activities. Kari and I were both very relaxed and free of any anxiety or stress. That felt very good and comforting.

Once again I faced the certainty of having no functioning GPS for the first part of our trip today so I had carefully planned the route using the VOR navigation aids that were available and well known to me. I also carefully reviewed charts so that safe and correct navigation was, I hoped, assured. We would go direct to the Goffs VOR and then turn towards the Hector VOR. After Hector we would head straight to the Palmdale and from Palmdale we could literally see our way back to Whiteman. Using the VOR's was easy, but identifying good solid ground references for pilotage navigation was a bit more daunting over the vast openness of the great Mojave Desert. Still I wanted all options available not so much because of any concern over eventually finding the Whiteman Airport but rather because along our route of flight today was the R-2501 Restricted Area. The R-2501 Restricted area was in effect from the surface all the way up to Flight Level 400 or about 40,000 feet MSL and during the hours of always. We could not climb above R-2501 and we really did not want to enter R-2501. Oh sure we could have contacted the appropriate air traffic control agency and had R-2501 been not in use we could have been cleared through it. But guess what all air traffic control facilities are staffed by human beings. Human beings all from time to time err I have learned. So while that option was available I preferred to simply avoid R-2501. Doing that required a reasonable level of navigation skill. For those reasons I prepared my navigational procedures as thoroughly as I knew how to prepare them.

This would be our very last take off on this amazing adventure. That realization struck both Kari and me as at once joyous and sad. It was Joyous because we would soon be home with our friends and family and sad because this great adventure would soon be over. Well that is always the way things work.

At approximately 7:25 AM I started the engine. We completed the pre departure checks and taxied to runway 16 at the Bullhead City Airport. The tower had not yet opened at the Bullhead City Airport so we looked all around the traffic pattern for any possible and potentially conflicting traffic. We also made a radio transmission into the blind alerting any possible traffic in the area that we were about to take runway 16 for an immediate right cross wind departure. We saw no other traffic and heard from no other traffic and there being nothing left for us to do here on the ground we lined up on runway 16 at the Bullhead City Airport and applied full power. At this much lower elevation of a mere 695 feet MSL our airspeed climbed quickly and we rapidly took to the air. We maintained runway heading briefly and then turned to our right crossing the Colorado River and flying right by the line of big hotel casinos that mark Laughlin, Nevada on the modern map. As we climbed the GPS which had been working on the ground blinked out. "Satellite Reception Lost" it said on the screen. Well I knew that was coming. No problem I just turned and intercepted the 075 degree radial off of the Goffs VOR, centered the needle and flew to the radio navigation aid. Cake. The Goffs VOR was only 30 nautical miles away and because of our lower ground speed while climbing it would, I had calculated take us about 22 minutes to get there.

Sure enough in just about 20 minutes the to/from indicator began to flutter indicating that we were just about directly over the Goffs VOR. In fact Kari looked out the window and saw the VOR facility on the ground almost directly beneath us. See this stuff; this voodoo radio magic really does work. Dang.

From the Goffs VOR to the Hector VOR our course changed from 255 degrees to 238 degrees. I made the heading change but continued to use the Goffs VOR out bound while dialing the Hector VOR on the number two navigation radio. The GPS remained blank but the VOR's were working exactly as advertised. The odds were clearly favoring our safe return to the Whiteman Airport. But then it happened.

I was constantly looking out the window both for any possible traffic that might present a conflict or danger and for landmarks that would confirm our position. Roughly half way between the Goffs VOR and the Hector VOR I briefly got a little disoriented. The sight picture just didn't seem right. There was supposed to be a railroad track slightly to my north. There appeared, however to be a railroad track slightly to my south. That was not what I was expecting. The inbound needle for the Hector VOR was actually deflected slightly to the right suggesting that I was a bit left of course, but if that had been true than the rail road tracks would appear definitely to my north and not to my south. This was truly weird. Looking ahead everything seemed right but nothing was yet sufficiently detailed to confirm that belief. The question became what to do? I made a compromise decision and steered just a couple degrees to my right in deference to the VOR indication. Also any conflict I might have with the restricted area would be to my left so a small correction to the right was I felt the prudent choice.

Suddenly my GPS came alive and it showed that I was actually about a half mile to the north of the correct course. That seemed very weird but it made a compelling argument. Now the fact of the matter is that we were flying on one of those highways in the sky, a Victor Airway known as Victor 8 – 210. Victor Airways by definition allow for a variation of 4 nautical miles either side of the centerline of the airway, so I was well within the allowed parameters. Still my momentary flash of confusion was displeasing. Had the GPS not come back my decision would have taken us well less than 4 miles north of the airway and for sure as we got closer to the Hector VOR additional course corrections could and would have been made. But this is the downside of VOR navigation, the VOR's themselves are not always totally dead on accurate and their signals do from time to time shift and vary. That is why using pilotage navigation is also a very good idea to stay absolutely aware of your position. The problem, however, with pilotage is that things on the ground do not always look like how they are depicted on the aeronautical charts. Oh those chart guys do a great job but charts are representations of the terrain and landmarks and not photographs.

All is well, they say, that ends well and my momentary bout of disorientation indeed ended quickly and well. Still the experience only reproved what I already knew and that is no matter how sophisticated our modern navigation aids happen to be, there remains the opportunity to still get confused or disoriented. So my earlier thought about how it is well nigh impossible for a general aviation pilot to get lost these days was perhaps a little bit overly optimistic. It is hard, but it is not impossible. But then it really makes you think about guys like Columbus who sailed successfully back and forth across the Atlantic Ocean with far less navigational assistance. Then there is Charles Lindbergh who miraculously flew over the Atlantic and found Paris, France with none of our modern tools. All I had to do was find the Whiteman

Airport a mere couple hundred miles the other side of this lousy

desert. What am I complaining about?

As we flew right on by the Hector VOR familiar sights came into

view. Just a wee bit to our north the Barstow – Daggett Airport

came into view and Kari and I discussed briefly how much fun we

had there. Up ahead not too far we would once again see the huge

Southern California Logistics Airport just to the south of our flight

path. Both Kari and I were totally relaxed now and she asked for

and was given control of the airplane. She did a perfect job of

holding heading and altitude for the better part of ten minutes. I

know a lot of licensed pilots who would struggle to do that. She

may never choose to become a pilot herself, nor would I even try

to push that upon her, but if that was her decision someday, I have

no doubt but that she would be a truly awesome pilot. She is one

cool character, call sign ICEGIRL. Move over Maverick.

We were quickly coming up on Palmdale; Whiteman Airport was not all that far away, about maybe 50 miles is all from right here and right now. So just for fun I dialed in 135.00 MHz on the communications radio and was amazed to actually hear one of the airplanes I knew from Whiteman call the Whiteman Tower. I could also plainly hear a steady stream of jets inbound to the McCarran Airport in Las Vegas calling Las Vegas Center on that same frequency. Now this was real fun in a strange way. "Whiteman tower Cessna 13818 Newhall Pass landing." "Las Vegas Center Southwest 1455 leaving 24 thousand for 16 thousand." Two hundred miles apart and completely oblivious to each other and we were eaves dropping on both ends. We had one very tall antenna and it was working very well.

As we crossed over the Palmdale Airport I began a steady descent out of 10,500 aiming as I did this just a little to my left to intercept the 14 Freeway. Now there is some sophisticated navigation, IFR,

261

I follow roads. We were getting very close, now less than 35 nautical miles from home. Our descent continued and in only a few more minutes I was able to receive the Whiteman Airport ATIS. The current information at Whiteman was identified as information Bravo. I noted that we had a change in the altimeter setting and I made the necessary correction. As was expected the winds were still calm and the runway of choice for VFR departures and landings was runway 12.

Now Kari wanted to make the first radio call to the Whiteman tower. It was easy enough but she wanted to be absolutely right so I dictated to her and she wrote down the magic language creating for herself a small script. "Whiteman Tower, Cardinal one three hotel kilo, Newhall Pass, inbound with Bravo" she repeated over and over. She had it nailed. Now all we had to do was get to the Newhall Pass. Our descent continued and we crossed below 6000 feet as we flew abeam the Agua Dulce Airport. "Is that the

Newhall Pass daddy?" Kari asked as she pointed directly at the Newhall Pass. "Yes it is Kari, good job" I replied. "And that is where you make the radio call" I continued. We talked about the various cue options and agreed upon a simple pointing of the finger at the correct moment. We were now in a flying broadcast booth and we motored on continuing our descent.

I wondered where Nenita was. Would she see us land? Was she standing by the place where we tied down our airplane, or was she up front on the grassy area? I wondered if she had even left the house yet. Kari and I discussed this briefly and we agreed that mom was probably still at home just getting ready to leave. Mom is an island girl, from the Philippines and as such she has never been driven by a clock. But eventually we would be there and she would show up and that was, after all, what really mattered. We were now descending below 4500 feet MSL with Magic Mountain at about our two o'clock and the Newhall Pass about at our eleven o'clock. Kari repeated her radio call for I would guess about the thirtieth time by now. She was determined to get it absolutely right.

Soon we were at 3500 feet and directly over the Newhall Pass and I gave her the cue. She immediately pushed the push to talk switch on her control yoke and said: "Whiteman Tower, Cardinal one three hotel kilo, Newhall Pass inbound with Bravo." Without as much as a nano second hesitation Joel, the Tower supervisor came back with the expected "Cardinal one three hotel kilo make straight in for runway one two, report a three mile final." Kari beamed brightly and so did her dad. "WILCO, one three hotel kilo" I quickly spoke into my microphone and we continued in bound dropping below 3000 feet MSL before reaching the south end of the San Fernando Reservoir and the Burbank Airport's "Charlie" airspace. There before us was the east end of the fabled San Fernando Valley. Well actually before us was pretty much the entire San Fernando Valley but we were aiming for a spot on the ground at the east end. Straight ahead of us now was the Whiteman Airport.

As we approached the three mile mark Whiteman tower cleared us to land on runway one two of the Whiteman Airport. "Cleared to land runway one two, one three hotel kilo" I quickly replied as I set up for landing. "Cowl flaps open" I called out to Kari as she immediately opened the cowl flaps. Darn she was good. Flaps twenty, speed 80 miles per hour, trim up, gear down and welded, fuel on both tanks, landing light on we were ready. We passed the 118 freeway and dropped below 1500 feet MSL, less than 500 feet above the ground and I added the last notch of flaps. I held it right on the center line as we crossed the numbers I reduced the sink rate by pitching up a bit and holding the plane level. Airspeed steadily reduced and the plane descended gently and finally I pitched up as we approached the ground. The main wheels squeaked on to the runway and I held the nose up allowing airspeed to rapidly bleed off until finally the nose wheel settled on to the runway. I had despite my best efforts been slightly fast on the approach so we let the airplane slow naturally without any significant braking action and got off the runway at the Delta taxiway. Normally I would not have accepted that and I would have taxied back for another spin in the pattern until I landed to my satisfaction, but that would not happen this day. Both Kari and I were pooped, and we were on the ground and we were staying there.

The tower told us to taxi to parking with them and I glanced at my watch. It was 9:36 AM. Darn that was good I thought. "Kari" I said "we are still the world's most on time airline." She smiled broadly as we headed for our parking space.

We did not see mom anywhere. Oh well, our guess had probably been right. Mom was probably still somewhere between our home and the airport. Well at least we would not have to wait for our luggage, just mom.

We stopped the airplane, turned off all the avionics and shut down the engine. We were home. Next we pushed the airplane into her parking spot and began affixing the tie down chains. My car was still right we had left it only it was extremely dirty after ten days of total neglect. And then Kari screamed with joy "Mom!" Sure enough there came Nenita walking towards us from the direction of the airport office. What a beautiful sight, what a beautiful woman, what a beautiful daughter, what a lucky guy I thought all at once. After Kari I got a hug. Ah heck, that's okay with me. Then Kari immediately began serenading mom with her Navajo flute and mom wasn't quite sure what to make of that. Nor was she real sure about her daughter and husband both covered as we were with various Indian items and both a bit on the dusty side. But by now we, Kari and I, both thought that our throats had been cut, we were so hungry.

We finished up with the airplane, placing everything from our trip into my car and then driving the short distance to Rocky's Restaurant. Honestly Rocky's food had never tasted so good. Kari couldn't stop talking about all the exciting places we had been and all the fun things we had done. Mom just sat there smiling her warm smile; me too. Clearly I had accomplished my mission; I had provided both Kari and myself with a real true adventure that we would both remember for the rest of our time on this planet. Surely some day Kari will look back on what we had done and hand the baton on to her children. That was part of it, of course, but so was the already powerful link that had grown even stronger between Kari and me as we lived this adventure together. To be sure there are bigger stories, greater adventures and more dangerous feats played out and yet to be done in this world of ours. But for Kari and me this will always be our great flying adventure together. We both thoroughly enjoyed it and thanks for coming along with us. We hope you enjoyed it almost as much as we did.

Post Action Debrief

L et's start with the numbers.   In a period of ten days we had

Traveled approximately 1200 nautical miles or approximately 1380 statute miles by air

We had actually viewed something in excess of 250,000 square miles given our flight altitudes and the awesome visibility we enjoyed all along our flight path.

Total flight time was a modest 12.9 hours, but that is as measured by our engine tachometer which starts recording time from engine start to engine shut down. Actual time in the sky was less; I would estimate perhaps something close to 11.5 actual in the sky hours.

That would give us an average speed of about 104 nautical miles per hour or roughly 120 stature miles per hour.

Do keep in mind that this includes our climbs which were high typically on this trip and that reduced our average speed as climb speeds in the Cessna, Cardinal are right around 80 to 90 miles per hour. Our best ground speed was 138 knots or about 158 statute miles per hour. That occurred when we were flying east bound with a tail wind.

Our longest flight segment was 1.9 hours tachometer time. It was also our final flight segment from Bullhead City, Arizona to Whiteman Airport, Los Angeles, California.

The number of times Kari took control of the aircraft in flight was three. The number of radio calls made by Kari was one.

The highest altitude we reached was 12,000 feet. The airport we landed at with the highest elevation was Durango La Plata County

Airport at 6685 feet MSL. The airport with the lowest elevation was the Bullhead City Airport, Arizona at a mere

695 feet MSL.

To do this we consumed 103 gallons of 100 low lead aviation gasoline and 1 quart of Aeroshell 100 weight motor oil. That is way less than the carbon foot print left by Al Gore when he jets around in his Gulfstream.

Our ground transportation took us another 350 or so statute miles. I did not figure the fuel consumption for our ground transportation.

We visited the states of California, Arizona, Utah, Colorado, New Mexico and Nevada which is more than 10% of the 50 United States of America.

The furthest we got from home was Durango, Colorado at only about 600 nautical miles. That is, of course, by air. Due to the many mountains along the way an automobile would require something in excess of 850 or so driving miles.

We took off and landed from the following airports:

Whiteman Airport, California WHP

Barstow – Daggett Airport, California DAG

Kingman Airport, Arizona IGM

Grand Canyon National Park Airport, Arizona GCN

Kayenta Airport, Arizona, Navajo Nation 0V7

Durango La Plata County Airport, Colorado DRO

Gallup Municipal Airport, New Mexico GUP

Sedona Airport, Arizona SEZ

Bullhead City Airport, Arizona IFP

Along the way we visited the towns, cities, landmarks and parks as

follows

Whiteman Airport, Pacoima, Los Angeles, California

Daggett, California

Barstow, California

Yermo, California

Peggy Sue's Nifty Fifties Diner

Calico Ghost Town

Kingman, Arizona

The Grand Canyon National Park

Kayenta, Arizona, Navajo Nation

Monument Valley, Utah, Navajo Nation

Goulding Lodge, Utah

Durango, Colorado

Silverton, Colorado

Gallup, New Mexico

Sedona, Arizona

Cottonwood, Arizona

Flagstaff, Arizona

Bullhead City, Arizona

Laughlin, Nevada

We did all of these things in just ten days.

Together Kari and I watched approximately 20 hours of
programming on the Disney Channel. Also I finished reading for

the third time the book *Final Approach* by John Nance and began to read the book *Saboteurs* by W.E.B. Griffin.

We also agreed that while the entire adventure was truly sensational, our favorite place was Kayenta and Monument Valley and our least favorite place was Gallup, New Mexico.

Dad's favorite quote from Kari on this adventure occurred as we drove up to Silverton, Colorado and she blurted out what she was reading on a road sign: "Road Damage!" Okay you had to be there but it was hilarious.

Finally two things that need to be wrapped up, whatever happened to Darren Baird and what ever happened to my heightened sense of anxiety?

Darren Baird is not a particularly patient man. In that regard we are very similar. He especially has no patience when he perceives that his time is being stupidly squandered and that is what he came to believe was happening at Sheble Aviation. However, he met a flight instructor at Sheble who taught instrument flying at his flight school in Medford, Oregon. Conversations were had and a deal was made and Darren drove off into the sunset heading for Medford, Oregon. He spent roughly a week in Medford during which time he logged about 20 hours of instrument instructional flight. No doubt this has advanced his level of instrument competence considerably but he did not receive his instrument rating. He returned to the greater Los Angeles area one day after Kari and I returned. He has already come up with his new plan of action which involves a fair amount of time on a flight simulator. Getting an instrument rating is typically much harder than it should be but for a whole bunch of reasons that do not actually involve the intricacies of instrument flight. More likely to make the process fairly long and always expensive are the relatively high turn over of qualified flight instructors and the ability to fly regularly enough for the instruction to take a firm hold on the student. As you may suspect the number one reason for flight instructors to be flight instructors is to build enough time to be of interest to the airlines or at the very least the charter companies. Once they do become interesting to charter operators or an airline they are gone and the hapless student gets to go shop for another instructor. Then there is the student. If instrument flight instruction is not done on a frequent and regular basis building the necessary skills can take literally forever.

My good friend Darren is a bright and committed guy. He will ultimately become a proficient instrument pilot and he will ultimately earn his instrument rating. I will help him along whenever and however I can but at the end of the day it is his call.

He will end up where he wants to be, with his head in the clouds. Good luck Darren.

Now as for my anxiety attacks, they began to fade as we turned the corner in Durango, Colorado and began our march back home. I love to fly and flying has never scared me. No I am not making a macho claim, merely a statement of fact. I can't stand on a tall building or walk across even a modest bridge because I do have acrophobia, but flying is a whole different story for me. That I take to like a duck takes to water. So what caused this sudden shift in my comfort level?

That is simple, a profound sense of loving care for my daughter distorted by run away maternal fear. . I never seriously doubted the successful outcome of our adventure, but unfortunately that positive attitude was not shared by Kari's mom. Some of mom's irrational but clearly real and deep concern spilled over unto me.

Kari and I would be on the ramp preflighting the airplane and Kari

would be talking with her mom on the cell phone. I would hear

Kari saying things such as: "Yes mom, we will be fine." "Mom it

is only a one hour flight today." "Yes mom dad checked the fuel,

he always checks the fuel." "Yes mom both wings are still

attached." "No mom the Indians aren't wearing war paint."

Alright she didn't say anything about Indians and war paint.

This stuff would stick in my subconscious and while sleeping the

kaleidoscope dream effect would distort and amplify everything

turning essentially meaningless concerns and statements in to full

blown worries.

Kari herself was a little tentative at first and most likely for the

same reasons I became somewhat rattled along the way. Good old mom was scared and by golly she was going to make sure we were scared too. No offense to mom, her fear was real to her I am certain. Anyhow both Kari and I shed that anxiety as each day passed. By the time we had reached the turning point in Durango, Colorado it was as they say in the air traffic control business not a factor.

But after all is said and done Kari and I had enjoyed one heck of an adventure, both of us had learned and enjoyed and grown together. Certainly we had highs and lows along the way, yet overall it was a huge success. Mission accomplished!